Billionaire

How the Worlds Richest Men and Women Made Their Fortunes

By Rebecca Robinson

Minute Help Press

www.minutehelp.com

© 2011. All Rights Reserved.

Table of Contents

- Abigail Johnson 4
- Alexei Mordashov 6
- Andrew Beal 8
- Armancio Ortega-Gaona 10
- Bernard Arnault 12
- Bill Gates 14
- Carl Icahn 16
- Carlos Slim Helu 18
- David Thomson 20
- Donald Bren 22
- Donald Trump 24
- Eike Batista 26
- George Kaiser 28
- George Lucas 29
- Gordon Moore 31
- Harold Hamm 33
- Henry Ross Perot 35
- James Goodnight 37
- James Jannard 39
- James Kennedy 41
- Jeff Bezos 43
- John Franklyn Mars 45
- John Menard 47
- John Paulson 49
- Karl Albrecht 51
- Lakshmi Mittal 52
- Larry Ellison 54
- Larry Page 56
- Lee Shau-Kee 58
- Leonardo Del Vecchio 60
- Li Ka Shing 62

- Liliane Bettencourt 64
- Mark Zuckerberg 66
- Michael Bloomberg 69
- Michael Dell 71
- Micky Arison 73
- Mukesh Ambani 75
- Patrick Soon-Shiong 77
- Phil Knight 79
- Ralph Lauren 81
- Richard Branson 83
- Robin Li 85
- Ron Burkle 87
- Rupert Murdoch 89
- Samuel Newhouse 92
- Sergey Brin 94
- Sheldon Adelson 96
- Stefan Persson 98
- Steve Jobs 100
- Vladimir Lisin 102
- Warren Buffett 104
- About Minute Help Press 106

Abigail Johnson

Abigail Johnson landed herself on the *Forbes* 500 list through good old-fashioned hard work—and family money. The President of the Personal and Workplace Investing arm of Fidelity Investments, which handles stock plans for employees, Abigail is worth a cool $11.3 billion, the 26th richest billionaire in the U.S. Fidelity handles a staggering sum of money each year, right around the $1.5 trillion mark. In line with the family dynasty, Abigail has all the right credentials—MBA from Harvard, Boston blood, and an insider's look at the family business. But she also knows how to work hard.

Abigail's grandfather, Edward C. Johnson II, founded the Fidelity Company in 1946 and the company boomed quickly. December 19, 1961, saw the birth of Abigail in the company's headquarters in Boston, MA. Five-year-old Abigail may not have even noticed when her father, Edward III, joined Fidelity in 1967 as a stock analyst. Ten years later, however, family life certainly changed when, in 1977, Edward III became the company's president.

Clearly, this is a group that likes to keep it all in the family. *Forbes* reports that over half of the Fidelity Company is owned by the Johnson family; Abigail has even made money by selling shares to her own family members. But grandfather Edward and father Edward weren't about to just hand their hard work over to a *woman*. They made her prove herself first.

Fresh out of high school, Abigail began at the bottom of the pack, starting her career answering phones in the customer-service department. Displaying a knack for well-rounded interests, Abigail chose to major in art history during her time at Hobart and Smith College. Her preference for contemporary art with clean and classic lines has even been compared to her work as an analyst and her success in the business place—careful and thorough, even traditional at times, but taking risks where necessary.

Following graduation from undergrad, she gained some experience as a research consultant with the management firm Booz Allen and Hamilton. After dutifully earning her MBA from Harvard's Business School, Abigail joined the old boys' club by following in her father's footsteps as a stock analyst for Fidelity in 1988, proving herself capable with slow and steady results tracking industrial equipment stocks. In 1993, she completed a successful run of her first diversified fund (a big deal in the stock market world). Her father, Edward III, relaxed the reins with Abigail's success, priming her for an upward climb through the company and passing down a 24% company inheritance to her. Her next promotion was to portfolio manager in 1988. Her business success as manager also coincided with personal success, as Abigail married Christopher John McKown, the President of Force Financial Services, that same year. Abigail later gave birth to two daughters.

While some may argue that the $10 billion fortune Abigail was destined to inherit could serve as a source of courage and comfort, the pressure to succeed could be suffocating. But Abigail kept her cool.

She continued her steady climb when she was named Fidelity's associate director in 1994 and then senior vice president in 1998. Three years later, in 2001, she became president of investment services. And finally, in 2005, Abigail took over as president of Fidelity's Employer Services Company.

Johnson is a rarity in the public eye, keeping a low profile and giving few interviews. She puts in long hours at the office and lives a low-key life close to her family outside of the office, where she is known as "Abby."

Fidelity Insight newsletter editor Eric Kobren summed up Abigail Johnson's approach to business and her personal life: "She's cool and calm, and she works hard every day." When featuring Abigail as one of the 100 most influential people in the world, *Time* magazine reported: "She doesn't have that air of being one of the richest people in the world." (http://www.time.com/time/magazine/article/0,9171,993990,00.html)

In 2011, Abigail's 81-year-old father announced his plans to step down from his position running Fidelity's fund boards. The move is scheduled to take effect in January 2012. Many people view Abigail as next in the line to the Fidelity throne.

• Alexei Mordashov

Self-made billionaire Alexei Mordashov hails from Russia. Mordashov's life is the quintessential rags-to-riches story. He was born in 1965, the only child of steel mill-worker parents in the late Soviet era in Cherepovets, a small steel town about 500 kilometers north of Moscow. Money didn't come easily to the family. With an electrician father and a maintenance worker mother, Mordashov and his family used food coupons to survive, measuring out sausage and butter to the allotted amounts. Mordashov vowed to overcome the Soviet system of communism, showing a passion for economics and graduating from the Leningrad Institute of Engineering and Economics in St. Petersburg, where he received a Bachelor of Arts and Science degree. After graduating from college, he gained employment and experience as a planning economist with Cherepovetskiy Metallurgical Plant, the same steel plant where his parents once worked. Ever the entrepreneur, Mordashov went on to earn his Master of Business Administration degree from Northumbria University in England via a correspondence program.

Mordashov made his money as the head honcho of the steelmaking company Severstal, based in Russia. As the CEO of Severstal, Russia's largest steelmaker, and one of the world's largest steel and mining companies, Mordashov enjoys his fortune of an estimated $9.9 billion (as of June 2010, reported by *Forbes*).

Still in his twenties, Mordashov joined Severstal as an assistant manager, learning while under the aegis of the company's current director Yuri V. Lipukhin. Mordashov deviated from much of the cultural norms of the business world in Russia, valuing Lipukhin's experience and learning from the older gentleman. Mordashov was quoted as saying, "At that time old experience wasn't considered worth anything, but young people were much more flexible."

Mordashov obviously thought otherwise. Working under Lipukhin, Mordashov shone and was soon promoted to finance director, landing himself in the right place at the right time. When the government privatized the company against the advice of many older workers who thought the shares were a waste of time and money, Mordashov bought up the flailing company's shares. As a manager with the inside access, he was able to scoop them up for his own personal use, then an accepted and legal practice in Russia. Buying the shares turned out to be, quite possibly, the smartest move of Mordashov's career. The combination of experience he found in his friend Lipukhin with Mordashov's youth and enthusiasm proved to be a winning combination. He soon controlled over half of the company's shares.

"I like that old Chinese proverb," said Mordashov in an interview with *The Sunday Times*. (http://business.timesonline.co.uk/tol/business/article664580.ece) "When the caravan turns around, the last camel becomes the first. That's me. I was last camel at the steel plant and I became the first because of the turnaround."

Even with the taste of this success still in his mouth, he looked for new ways to make money in the Russian steel market. Showing a flair for management and a gift for profit, Mordashov was named the company's new general director in 1996 at the tender age of thirty. He wasted no time, digging in immediately to restructure the company. First he tackled manager accountability, establishing "cost and profit" centers to train and evaluate managers' actions for the company. He hired international consultants to provide independent advice for improving the company's image, efficiency, and profits. Creating a massive infrastructure, Mordashov expanded beyond the company's main inventory of steel and invested in other industries, such as mining, auto and even television industries. In what was probably a happy day for Mordashov, the company consolidated other steel and mining plants, including the same plant he and his parents had once worked at. Lastly, he took drastic measures to cut costs, reducing Severstal's employee count from 53,000 to 38,000.

Mordashov proved himself a capable and involved director, and profits soon soared. Whatever he touched turned to gold. Following Mordashov's restructuring plan, Severstal boasted sales clearing $1.93 billion. Six years later, Mordashov became chairmen of the board of Severstal.

Like many top billionaires in the world, Mordashov is a man of few words. He summed up his company's success in a 2007 article for *Forbes* magazine: "We make a lot of money."
(http://www.*Forbes*.com/*Forbes*/2007/1210/108.html)

You got that right, Mordashov.

• Andrew Beal

Michigan-born and -raised billionaire Andrew Beal (worth around $6.6 billion in March 2011, according to *Forbes*) is a man of many talents. Unlike other amateur billionaires who rely on one source of wealth to provide their incomes, Beal made his money in the banking and real estate markets while also founding Beal Bank and Beal Aerospace Technologies. An aptitude for math and a confident approach has also served him well in his other interest: high-stakes poker games.

Born on November 11, 1952, in Lansing, Michigan, Beal began as an entrepreneur of sorts under the tutelage of his uncle. As the son of a mechanical engineer, Beal inherited his father's affinity for working with his hands. Beal and his uncle fixed broken television sets, selling them for a profit to low-income families after the repairs. Moving on to bigger projects, Beal enlisted the help of his friends in a business venture re-positioning homes; the teens would use hydraulic lifts to raise houses from their foundations, move them, and then level the homes correctly. (Yes, he and his friends were still in their teens when they moved and leveled houses.)

Beal enrolled at Michigan State University, where he continued flexing his business muscles. At only 19, he became a homeowner, purchasing his first house in the Lansing area for $6,500. After leaving Lansing and moving on to Baylor University in Texas, Beal began renting the home for $119 a month, thus scoring his first big profit as a businessman. Beal never finished his degree at Baylor, making him a billionaire college dropout.

The secret to Beal's success appears to be in his willingness to dig in and try new moneymaking ventures. After his first real estate gain, Beal began building his billions by purchasing more down-and-out properties, starting with the Brick Towers, a project building in New Jersey. He was able to turn a profit in real estate, which then enabled him to open his first bank in Dallas in 1988. The bank did well, even after Beal's unsuccessful attempts to expand business into foreign markets such as Russia and Mexico. Beal opened a second branch in Nevada a few years later.

He continued his business attempts, next reaching for the stars with a start-up aerospace company meant to build rockets for satellite placement. Beal Aerospace was founded in the mid-90s to compete with NASA and other leading satellite-launching companies. However, proving that risk can indeed be risky, the company never turned a profit and closed after three years of financial loss.

Undaunted, Beal next saw an opportunity after the 9-11 attacks, buying up airlines' debt at low prices following the attacks and selling them for huge profits. Beal continues to make money off the airline bonds to this day.

So yes, Beal is good at business. But he also happens to be a very fine poker player. Displaying an affinity for gambling and a love of poker, Beal once won $11.7 million in a single poker game. Other successful poker games resulted in a $13.3 million win over a succession of three days in 2006. He is known as a legend of sorts for the game he played at the Las Vegas Bellagio in 2001 when he challenged the world's greatest poker players to a game with a $2 million hand—the highest stakes in the casino's history. Although he lost more than he won that day, the image of Beal—calm, cool, and playing the money market on his own terms—remains.

His more recent strategies include gathering loans from cash-strapped banks, starting in 2004. Beal seemed to know the blows were going to come. Then when the recession hit in 2007, he stopped his massive loan buying. While other creditors and lenders bought into the loan-heavy craze, Beal laid low. Fearing that the loans were about to crumble, Beal reduced costs by cutting employees and keeping bank business to a minimum. His seemingly puzzling behavior paid off when the loans went south—and his stayed safe. Beal was able to stay free of federal intervention, tripling his bank's assets up to $7 billion the year the recession hit. He bought up more than $800 million of failed bank loans, proving that sometimes, patience plays out.

Armancio Ortega-Gaona

Armancio Ortega-Gaona is a Spanish entrepreneur. He is ranked by *Forbes* as the richest person in Spain, the second richest in Europe, and the seventh richest in the world.

Ortega was born on March 28, 1936, in Busdongo de Arbas, Spain, the son of a railway worker. He has been married twice, first to Rosalía Mera, also a billionaire, whom he divorced. He is currently married to Flora Pérez Marcote, with whom he resides in A Coruña, Spain. Ortega has two daughters, Sandra Ortega Mera and Marta Ortega Pérez, and a son, Marcos Ortega Mera.

At the age of 14, Ortega's family moved to A Coruña, Galicia. While there he began his career by working as a delivery boy for a men's shirt store that served wealthy people and as an assistant in a tailor's shop. Through this work he learned about the costs of manufacturing and delivering clothing directly to customers. He later became manager of a clothing store with a wealthy clientele similar to that of the men's shirt store.

In 1972, Ortega founded Confecciones Goa (his three initials in reverse), which manufactured bathrobes, lingerie, and dressing gowns. Ortega began simply, sewing his products in his living room.

In 1975 Ortega opened the first store in the popular fashion chain, Zara, in A Coruña, selling trendy clothing for men and women. Zara soon became the cornerstone of the Inditex (Industrias de Diseño Textil Sociedad Anónima) group. In only five years, Inditex doubled in size, with 2001 sales of $2.3 billion and a net of $233 million. About 80 per cent of its sales come from the flagship Zara chain.

Other companies owned by Inditex include Massimo Dutti, Oysho, Zara Home, Kiddy's Class, Tempe, Stradivarius, Pull and Bear/Often and Bershka.

On May 23, 2001, Ortega went public with Inditex on the Madrid Stock Exchange, earning $10 billion overnight and suddenly vaulting him to the top of the list of Spain's richest people. At the time, the company owned five clothing store chains with more than 1,000 stores in 34 countries. Since that time, Inditex has grown to an empire of over 4,500 stores in 73 different countries.

In 2010 Ortega set up a joint venture with the Tata Group subsidiary to enter the clothing market in India. Other countries in which Inditex has stores include Mexico and Syria.

Ortega has also invested in real estate, recently purchasing the Coral Gables, Florida, office tower that houses the offices of Bacardi USA. Other real properties owned by Ortega include a luxury apartment complex in Miami as well as real estate in Paris, Lisbon, Madrid, and London.

In addition to textiles and real estate, Ortega also owns interests in a horse-jumping circuit, tourist operations, banks, gasoline, and even a soccer league.

Ortega likes to dress in blue jeans and T-shirts and never wears ties.

The reclusive Ortega lives very simply and privately in a modest apartment building in A Coruña and refuses to give interviews. There are very few pictures of him, even on the Internet.

Even at the age of 75, Ortega continues to take an active part in the company's production and design processes, although he has recently announced that he plans to retire from Inditex in the near future. He has said that he will ask Inditex vice-president and CEO Pablo Isla to take over as CEO of the textile empire, but speculation is that his daughter, Marta, who currently works for Inditex, will some day replace her father as CEO.

Bernard Arnault

Bernard Arnault was born on March 5, 1949, in the town of Roubaix in northern France. Arnault's mother, a classical pianist, saw to it that he, too, learned to play classical piano including works by Frederich Chopin and Franz Liszt. This early artistic training instilled in him a love of art and luxury.

Arnault received a B.A. from the École Polytechnique in 1971.

Upon graduation, Arnault joined his family's company, Ferret-Savinel, as an engineer. In 1976, Arnault convinced his father to sell off the company's construction division and move the company into the real estate business. The sale brought 40 million francs, which the company used to become one of the first companies to build time-shares on the French Riviera under its new name of Férinel.

When Francois Mitterand and the Socialists came into power in France in 1981, Arnault moved to the United States and established the U.S. branch of the family business, Ferinel, Inc. He began developing condos and an apartment complex with a limited partnership in West Palm Beach, Florida. Unfortunately, the complex defaulted on its mortgage almost as soon as it was completed. The investors lost all of the money they had invested and the bondholders lost most of theirs.

In 1983, after the Socialists became more conservative, Arnault returned to France and became CEO of luxury goods maker Financière Agache.

When textile manufacturer Boussac declared bankruptcy, Arnault, with backing from his friend Antoine Bemheim of investment company Lazard Frères, purchased Boussac. The Arnault family invested $15 million, while Lazard paid the remainder of the rumored $80 million purchase price.

At the time, Boussac owned businesses as diverse as a disposable diaper company and the once-revered House of Christian Dior. Arnault wanted Boussac primarily for Dior, which he saw as the foundation of a luxury-goods empire. He sold everything except Dior Couture and Le Bon Marché department stores but added Christian Lacroix fashions and Celine, which manufactures leather goods including a high-fashion line of loafers.

Arnault used the proceeds from the divestiture of Boussac's non-luxury lines to purchase $1.8 billion worth of Moët Hennessy Louis Vuitton (LVMH) shares, giving him control of 24 percent of the business. LVMH owned the rights to Dior perfumes, which Arnault wanted to add to Dior Couture. After the stock market crash of 1987, Arnault took advantage of depressed stock prices to buy an additional 21% of LVMH.

Arnault took advantage of the conflict between Moët Hennessy's CEO Alain Chevalier and Louis Vuitton's president Henri Racamier. Arnault won a series of bitter court battles that ousted Racamier, a member of one of Louis Vuitton's founding families. He then proceeded to purge all of LVMH's top Vuitton executives and installed his father, Jean Leon Arnault, as chairman of the board before he, himself, took over in 1989 as Chairman and CEO. Arnault's takeover of LVMH and his subsequent firing of the executives earned him a reputation among some people as a brutal businessman, but others respected his business strategy and risk tolerance.

During the 1990s, Arnault bought dozens of luxury-goods manufacturers throughout Europe, Asia, Australia, and the Americas. He added winemakers and liquor distilleries as well as Louis Vuitton luggage and Givenchy clothes and perfume. He bought watchmaker TAG Heuer, *Art and Auction* magazine, and cosmetics giant Sephora.

Arnault has the rare combination of being able to relate to and balance the creative and financial aspects of business. In 1995 Arnault fired the heads of Dior perfumes and a top manager at Givenchy due to their failure to produce profits and replaced them with executives from the U.S. who were not in the fashion industry. The new executives made changes that were unpopular but ultimately profitable, including changing aspects of some products that had been thought to be iconic. The changes resulted in making these products seem both timeless and up-to-date.

In the late 1990s, despite warnings from some investors and competitors who thought he was becoming too diversified, Arnault continued to amass luxury goods manufacturers such as Prada and Fendi. These sales failed to realize the anticipated profits when sales flatted and margins fell. Additionally, companies in the retail division, including an auction house and duty-free airport shops, were just barely profitable.

In 2001 many analysts cut their recommendation for LVMH from "buy" to "neutral". Because of the cut, decreased operating margins, and the failure of results to match expectations, Arnault finally stopped buying to concentrate on generating cash. LVMH sold its interest in the Phillips auction house and divested itself of a few other unprofitable divisions.

In the late 2000s, Arnault resumed acquisitions, including 10% of Carrefour, France's largest supermarket chain. Other holdings include Dom Perignon, Hermes, Bulgari, yacht builder Royal Van Lent, and French tour operator Go Voyages.

Today Arnault ranks fourth on *Forbes*' list of the world's richest people and first on the list of richest Europeans with a 2011 net worth estimated at $41 billion. He has been awarded the French Legion of Honor for his success in business.

Arnault is married to his second wife, Canadian concert pianist Helene Mercier. He has three sons and two daughters. He enjoys collecting art and has created the Louis Vuitton Foundation for Creation. The foundation's Frank Gehry-designed headquarters is scheduled to open at the Jardin d'Acclimatation in 2012.

• Bill Gates

Bill Gates was born William Henry Gates III on October 28, 1955, in Seattle, Washington. He was the middle child (between two sisters) of William H. Gates, Sr., a prominent attorney, and mother Mary Maxwell Gates. Mary, the daughter of a bank president, gave up her career as a teacher to concentrate on raising her family and charitable and civic duties, including serving on the board of directors of First Interstate Bank, the United Way, and IBM.

The Gates family was close and extremely competitive. Bill organized sports games and competitions at the family's summer house on Puget Sound. He also loved to play competitive board games such as Risk and Monopoly. Bill's other childhood activities included sports and Scouting.

Gates currently lives in Medina, WA, with wife Melinda, a former Microsoft employee whom he married in 1994, and their three children, Jennifer Katharine, Rory John, and Phoebe Adele.

Gates became interested in computers when the Mothers' Club at his exclusive prep school, the Lakeside School, purchased a Teletype Model 33 ASR terminal and a block of computer time on a General Electric (GE) computer with proceeds from a rummage sale. The school revoked Gates' and his close friend Paul Allen's computer privileges when they discovered the pair exploiting software bugs to get free computer time from GE. After their probation, the boys offered to debug the program in exchange for more free computer time. Gates subsequently developed a scheduling program for the school (which he used to place himself into classes that held a majority of girls) and a payroll system for the computer company whose bugs he exploited. He also developed traffic-counting systems for local governments.

In 1973, Gates headed off to Harvard University intending to become a lawyer like his father. His intentions went by the wayside when, in 1975, he and Allen read an article in Popular Mechanics on the Altair 8800, an inexpensive microcomputer being manufactured in New Mexico by the MITS company. Gates and Allen entered into a deal with MITS to develop software for the Altair. At the tender age of 19, Gates and Allen founded the Micro-Soft (later changed to Microsoft) Corporation in Albuquerque. The company moved to Bellevue, WA, on January 1, 1979.

Gates and Allen later entered into a partnership with IBM to develop an operating system for the new IBM Personal Computer (PC). They bought the rights to an existing software package and converted it to run on the PC. That system became known as MS-DOS (Disk Operating System). Eventually, MS-DOS and Microsoft's other programs (including Windows, Internet Explorer, and the Office Suite of software programs) helped Microsoft become the largest producer of microcomputer software in the world.

In the early years, Gates continued to actively develop software and write code. Gates' hands-on approach and aggressive management style, coupled with the competitiveness he learned as a child, earned him a reputation as a shrewd and ruthless leader.

In the late 1980s, Microsoft's spiraling stock prices helped Gates become a billionaire at age 31 and eventually propelled him to the top of *Forbes*' list of the world's richest people; he was the youngest self-made millionaire in history and the epitome of the wealthy computer geek, with a net worth of $1.25 billion.

Beginning in 1995, Gates changed Microsoft's focus to developing software for Internet and computer hardware such as the Xbox.

In 1997 the U.S. Justice Dept. accused Microsoft of violating an antitrust agreement, because the Windows operating system requires users to load Internet Explorer, thereby giving Microsoft a monopoly over other browses. The judge ruled that Microsoft violated the Sherman Antitrust Act and ordered that Microsoft break up into two companies. The company appealed and an appeals court overturned the breakup but agreed that Microsoft had stifled competition and returned the case to a lower court. Eventually Microsoft forged a settlement with the U.S. government, but the European Union continued to fine the company.

In response to criticism that he should do more philanthropic work, Gates created a charitable foundation that is known today as the Bill and Melinda Gates Foundation. For their philanthropic activities, Time magazine named Bill and Melinda Gates, along with U2's Bono, its Persons of the Year for 2005. In 2006 Gates stepped down from everyday operations at Microsoft to devote his time to the foundation, which focuses on health and education issues. He remains as Microsoft's chairman.

Gates' other business interests include Corbis (a digital imaging company) and acting as a director of Warren Buffett's Berkshire Hathaway. He is also CEO of Cascade Investment.

Among Gates' personal acquisitions is the Codex Leicester, a collection of writings by Leonardo da Vinci, which Gates bought for $30.8 million at an auction in 1994.

As of 2011, Gates' net worth is estimated at $56 billion. He is currently ranked second on the list of the world's wealthiest people.

• Carl Icahn

Carl Celian Icahn amassed his fortune as an American corporate raider and investor, although he calls himself a "shareholder activist".

Icahn was born February 16, 1936, in Queens, New York. He was raised in a middle-class Jewish-American home. His mother was a teacher and his father a cantor. He has been married twice and has two children.

Icahn graduated from Princeton with a degree in psychology. He briefly attended New York University School of Medicine but dropped out to pursue a career in business, joining Dreyfus & Company as a stockbroker in 1961.

In 1968, he bought a seat on the New York Stock Exchange with borrowed money and formed a securities firm, Icahn & Co., which was involved in arbitrage and options trading.

A decade later he began amassing majority shares in corporations as diverse as Texaco, Nabisco, and U.S. Steel. In 1985 he staged a hostile takeover of TWA that became legendary. Icahn has also profited greatly from following the teachings of junk bond king Michael Milken.

Icahn's mode of operation is to buy large or majority stakes in companies and then attempt to obtain a seat on the board of directors. Once ensconced, he tries to make the company more profitable, usually by slashing costs. Failing that, he attempts to overthrow the company's leaders and sell the company to the highest bidder.

In 2008, Icahn participated in the attempted takeover of Yahoo! and the ousting of then-CEO Jerry Yang so Microsoft could buy the company. He then agreed to join Yahoo's Board of Directors in a deal that would end the proxy fight. A year later, he resigned from the board and subsequently reduced his equity stake to 12 million shares.

In June 2008, Icahn launched The Icahn Report, which campaigns for shareholder rights.

At one time Icahn held interests in several Las Vegas and Laughlin, NV, hotels and casinos, including the iconic Stratosphere. In 2008, he sold them for $1.3 billion, about $1 billion more than he had originally paid. He currently owns and is in the process of renovating property in Las Vegas.

Icahn also attempted to take over Time Warner. At one time he held a little over 3% of the company's stock and proposed breaking the company up into four parts. Eventually he and his cohort agreed not to contest the re-election of the existing board members in exchange for Time Warner's buy-back of $20 billion of stock and cost-cutting measures totaling $1 billion.

He has been accused of illegally depressing stock prices in order to make companies private cheaply.

Despite his sometimes questionable tactics, Icahn has a philanthropic side. He contributes to the Carl C. Icahn Center for Science and the Icahn Scholar Program at Choate Rosemary Hall, a New England prep school. This organization funds full scholarships for ten students every year.

Icahn has also contributed a large donation to Princeton University to fund the Carl C. Icahn Laboratory at the Institute for Integrated Genomics. He has also given large contributions to Mount Sinai Hospital, funds the

Children's Rescue Fund, and built the Icahn House for homeless women and their children, as well as two additional shelters for the homeless of New York.

In 1985, Icahn began investing in and breeding thoroughbred racehorses. His horse, Meadow Star, won the 1990 Breeders' Cup Juvenile Fillies race and the Eclipse Award for Outstanding Two-Year-Old Filly. In 2004 he sold all of his female horses at auction.

Icahn's ruthless attitude towards business dealings is evident in his often-quoted saying, "If you want a friend, get a dog."

Icahn's 2011 net worth is estimated at $12.5 billion, ranking him 61st on the list of richest people in the world and the 23rd richest American.

Carlos Slim Helu

Carlos Slim Helu is a Mexican business magnate and founder of Grupo Carso.

Slim was married to Soumaya Domit Gemayel until her death in 1999. Their six children are Carlos, Marco Antonio, Patrick, Soumaya, Vanessa and Johanna.

Slim was born in Mexico City on January 28, 1940. His father, Khalil Slim Haddad, who later changed his name to Julián, was a Lebanese immigrant who entered Mexico at the age of 14. Julián and his brother, José, founded a dry goods store, La Estrella de Oriente ("the Star of the East"), that became worth more than $100,000 by 1921,

To teach them how to manage their income and expenses, Don Julián gave each of his six children a savings book with their weekly allowance. Carlos learned well, opening his first checking account and buying shares of Banco Nacional de México when he was only 12 years old. Don Julian died unexpectedly when Carlos was only 13.

Carlos went on to graduate from the National Autonomous University of Mexico with a degree in civil engineering.

After graduation, Slim formed Inversora Bursátil and became chairman. He next acquired Jarritos del Sur and incorporated Inmobiliaria Carso. This was the foundation for Grupo Carso, whose name was a combination of Carlos and Soumaya, his then-fiancee. Carlos and Soumaya were married the following year.

Slim next founded real estate company Promotora del Hogar and construction equipment company GM Maquinaria. Other companies that Slim acquired during that time include mining and investment firms as well as a majority of printing company Galas de México.

Grupo Carso is also invested in retail, tobacco, hotels, and food companies. He also owns all or part of General Tire, Reynolds Aluminio, Firestone, and British American Tobacco, as well as Seguros de México. He subsequently folded Seguros de México, Fianzas La Guardiana, and Casa de Bolsa Inbursa into one operation called Grupo Financiero Inbursa. This group now includes Fábricas de Papel Loreto y Peña Pobre, Pamosa, Sanborn's, Denny's, Artes Gráficas Unidas, and 50% of Hershey's.

In 1990, Slim took Grupo Carso public. Grupo Carso eventually was split into three companies: Carso Global Telecom, Grupo Carso and Invercorporación.

Slim entered the telecommunications business in 1990 with the acquisition of TELMEX in partnership with Southwestern Bell and France Telecom. In 1997, TELMEX began operating in the U.S. Slim later extended his telecommunications interests with shares in U.S. cell phone company Tracfone and further cemented his position when he established América Telecom, the holding company for América Móvils and acquired an equity stake in cell phone companies throughout South America. Slim and TELMEX partnered with Microsoft CEO Bill Gates to launch the Spanish portal T1msn (today ProdigyMSN), which soon became the leading portal in Mexico. From 2000 through 2006, Slim continued to acquire telecommunications companies and partners, including AT&T Latin America and Embratel, Brazil's leading telecom company.

In the retail area, Slim owns the majority of or holds interests in Sears and Roebuck and Saks Incorporated. In publishing, Slim owns interests in The New York Times Company.

He has served as vice chairman of the Mexican Stock Exchange and Chairman of the Mexican Association of Brokerage Firms. He was the first chairman of the Latin American Committee of the board of directors of the New York Stock Exchange.

Slim is now semi-retired; his sons Carlos, Marco, and Patrick have taken over much of his businesses.

Slim is not immune to criticism. His fortune has caused controversy because it has been earned in a country in which the average annual income is less than $14,500 a year and almost 17% of the population lives below the poverty level. Others criticize Slim for holding monopolies such as TELMEX, which controls 90% of Mexico's landline telephone market and charges among the highest usage fees in the world.

Slim has established several non-profit foundations including Fundación Carlos Slim Helú, which supports health, education, and sports programs; and the Fundación TELMEX which supports education, health, nutrition, justice, culture, environmental, sports, and disaster relief.

Slim has also established the Fundación del Centro Histórico de la Ciudad de México, whose goal is to restore and revitalize Mexico City's famous Zona Rosa historic district.

Several projects initiated by Slim's late wife, Soumaya, are still active, including an organization that supports organ donation.

The Slims also established the Museo Soumaya art museum that houses over 64,000 works by artists such as Rodin and Dali and conducts research, conservation and promotion of Mexican and European art.

The Embassy of Lebanon has awarded Slim The National Order of the Cedar and Fundación TELMEX has received the National Sports Award.

Slim was named Man of the Year in 2008 by the World Boxing Council.

Slim enjoys history, art, and nature and is a baseball aficionado who has written several articles on the subject.

Slim sits atop *Forbes'* list of the richest people in the world with a net worth estimated at $74 billion.

• David Thomson

David Thomson is a Canadian media magnate and businessman with the inherited title of Third Baron Thompson of Fleet. He is also co-chair with his brother Peter of the family's investment business, Woodbridge.

Thomson is chairman of Thomson Reuters and of the TR Organization, as well as co-chairman of the Woodbridge Company.

Thomson is divorced and has four children. Two daughters were born while he was married to his ex-wife. His son was born after he left his ex-wife. That son is the prospective heir to Thomson's fortune. He also has one daughter born out of wedlock to actress Kelly Rowland.

Thomson was born on June 12, 1957, in Ontario, Canada, of English and Scottish descent. His parents were Nora Marilyn Lavis Thomson and Kenneth Thomson, the Second Baron Thomson of Fleet. He has three siblings: brother Peter Thomson, sister Shirley Thomson, and actress Taylor Thomson.

David's career path was decided for him decades ago by his grandfather, Roy Thomson, who founded Thomson Corporation in 1934 and insisted that his sons and grandsons take responsibility for the family business and fortune.

Thomson attended Upper Canada College and earned a Master of Arts in history from both Selwyn College and the University of Cambridge.

Thomson then proceeded to work at various positions in his family's companies. He became manager of The Bay store at Cloverdale Mall in Etobicoke, Canada, and President of Zellers. In 2002 he took over from his father as chairman of Thomson Corporation.

He then founded a real estate firm named Osmington Incorporated, which he owned and operated on his own, separate from the Thomson Company holdings. Osmington is a partner in True North Sports and Entertainment, which recently purchased the Atlanta Thrashers of the National Hockey League, moved the franchise to Winnipeg (making them Canada's seventh NHL team), and renamed the team the Winnipeg Jets. True North also owns and operates the MTS Centre sports arena in downtown Winnipeg, Manitoba.

David's father, Kenneth, passed away in 2006. On June 12, David's 49th birthday, he inherited the family fortune, control of the family business, and the title of Third Baron Thomson of Fleet.

Recently the media conglomerate has moved away from printed material and into software and electronic media, such as Westlaw, a research tool for the legal profession.

Thomson and his ex-wife had a particularly bitter and nasty divorce. David left his wife when she was pregnant with their second child and took up with actress Rowland, who is best known for her role on the The O.C. Thomson and Rowland became engaged but he broke off the engagement just before Rowland gave birth to their child, a daughter.

An avid art collector, Thomson is a patron of the Art Gallery of Ontario. He owns the world's best collection of paintings by John Constable. At a 2008 art auction, the family bought $5 million worth of native North American art, including a $1.8 million facemask. It was the highest amount to date ever spent on one piece of native North American art. At the time David stated that the family bought the collection in honor of their father.

He is an advocate of living a balanced life and enjoys spending time with family and friends. Like most Canadian citizens and residents, he is also an avid ice hockey fan.

Thomson is extremely averse to publicity and has rarely agreed to be interviewed.

With a net worth approaching an estimated $23 billion Canadian, David Thompson is the richest person in Canada and ranks 16th on the Forbes list of the richest people in the world.

• Donald Bren

Donald Bren is the wealthiest real estate developer in the United States. His father, Milton Bren, was a famed movie producer; his mother, Marion Jorgensen, was a prominent socialite and philanthropist. He is married to Brigitte Muller and has seven children. Bren is the sole owner of the Irvine Company, a real estate development company located in the heart of Orange County, California. He is also part owner of the Mission Viejo Company. His net worth is estimated to be somewhere around $12 billion. He is the wealthiest resident of Southern California—no small feat.

Despite his immense wealth, his name is more commonly associated with his philanthropy than his business endeavors. Donald Bren has given hundreds of millions of dollars to K-12 and higher education programs. He has entire university schools named after him, such as the Bren School of Environmental Science and Management, a graduate school at UC Santa Barbara; and the Donald Bren School of Information and Computer Sciences at UC Irvine. (Both schools are among the best in their respective fields.)

He is also a trustee at the California Institute of Technology and has donated at least $10 million to the school in the past decade. He recently gave $20 million to help establish the UC Irvine School of Law. In addition, public schools in the city of Irvine, California, are some of the finest in the nation, thanks in large part to donations he made to the Irvine Unified School District.

In March 2009, he was ranked number nine by *The Sunday Times* (London) in their list of the world's most environmental-friendly persons of extreme wealth. His contributions to the environment include nearly 100,000 acres of park space and wilderness reserves that he donated to Orange County, as well as his $20 million donation to his namesake environmental science school at UCSB.

Bren attended the University of Washington on a skiing scholarship and received a bachelor's degree in business administration. He was supposed to compete in the 1956 Winter Olympics but could not qualify due to an untimely injury. After he graduated from college, he served in the United States Marine Corps for two years.

Bren got his start in the Orange County real estate market in 1958, when he built his first house in Newport Beach with a $10,000 loan. That same year, he founded Bren Company, which built homes throughout Orange County. In 1963, he and two others started the Mission Viejo Company and purchased 10,000 acres of land in what would one day become the city of Mission Viejo, a middle- to upper-class community in South Orange County. Bren was named president of the company, which essentially developed the entire city. Bren then sold the Mission Viejo Company in 1970, buying it back just two years later for $12 million less than its 1970 sales price.

Bren then resold the company in order to join a group of investors who wanted to purchase the Irvine Company. In that process, Bren became the Irvine Company's largest shareholder, owning roughly 1/3 of the company's shares. Over the years, he bought more and more shares, until in 1996 he finally became the company's only shareholder and thus its owner.

Many people rightfully consider him to be the master planner of the cities of Mission Viejo and Irvine. The Los Angeles Times once wrote, "Simply put, Orange County looks like Orange County—much of it uniformly manicured and catering to the high life and high tech—because of the influence of Bren."

On his investment strategy, Bren has said the following: "What I learned was that when you hold property over the long term, you're able to create better values and you have something tangible to show for it." Currently, Bren owns over 40 million square feet of office space and nearly 50,000 apartments throughout Southern California.

Bren is #64 on the *Forbes* list of the richest people in the world.

• Donald Trump

Donald Trump was born on June 14, 1946, to wealthy real estate investor and developer Fred Trump and his wife Mary Ann MacLeod.

Trump has been married three times and has five children.

An extramarital affair resulted in his first divorce and second marriage and was highly publicized. Trump's first wife, Ivana, encountered Trump's mistress, Marla Maples, while skiing in Aspen. Rumors had been circulating for some time that Maples and Trump had been involved. Ivana Trump filed divorce papers shortly after the confrontation with her husband's mistress. Donald Trump then married Maples not long after his divorce from Ivana was finalized. His first marriage lasted 15 years, and his marriage to Maples lasted less than five. Trump is now married to Melania Knauss, who is nearly a quarter-century younger than he.

At 13, Trump struggled at Kew-Forest School and was then sent to the New York Military Academy. There he earned honors in academics and played three different varsity sports throughout his stay. After graduating from the academy, he went straight to college. He first attended Fordham University, but transferred to the Wharton School and earned his bachelor's degree in economics there. While still in college, Trump began taking on projects for his father's real estate company. After graduation, Trump immediately returned home in order to work full-time for the family real estate business.

Trump saw much success early in his career, first following his father's niche, primarily focusing on middle-class rentals. By the early 1970s Trump had been convinced of the enormous wealth opportunity that Manhattan had to offer real estate developers. He began working on several projects in Manhattan, and was very successful throughout the 1970s and early 1980s. At the age of 25, he took over his father's company, The Trump Organization.

His early success would not carry him through the recession of 1991. By 1989 his debt was mounting. After he financed the construction of Trump Plaza Hotel's Taj Mahal in Atlantic City with junk bonds, he was unable to pay back construction loans. In the midst of recession, he was forced to file for business bankruptcy and was barely able to avoid personal bankruptcy by restructuring his debt. In 1992, Trump Plaza filed for Chapter 11 bankruptcy protection, and 49% of the luxury hotel was sold to outside investors. As a side note, Trump was successfully sued for $2 million by an outside analyst, who correctly predicted the inevitable bankruptcy of the Trump Plaza in 1990. After reading the prediction, Trump asked the analyst to retract his statements, but the analyst refused to do so. The analyst was fired soon after, the result of coercion on Trump's part. The lawsuit officially accused Trump of defamation, and the analyst also successfully sued his former employer for wrongful termination in the amount of $750,000. The fact that the analyst's prediction came true didn't hurt his case.

Since then, Trump has returned to his financially successful ways. Although he almost always claims to be worth more than others estimate, his net worth is assumed to be anywhere between $750 million and $3 billion. Trump recently lost a libel lawsuit he filed against another analyst, who estimated Trump's net worth to be below $250 million.

In 2003, Trump and his siblings sold their late father's real estate empire for $600 million. Trump's share of the company was $200 million. Despite the sale of his father's company, Trump remains very active in real estate.

He has also taken to more general investments. He owns a 17.2% stake in holding company Parker Adnan, among many others.

In addition to his continuing endeavors in the real estate and investment businesses, Trump has been known to dabble in an array of other side projects. In the late 1980s he was the owner of the USFL franchise the New Jersey Generals. He is also known for his love of professional wrestling. At one time he was Mike Tyson's primary financial advisor, and he has hosted a handful of major wrestling events, notably two WWE WrestleMania events at the Taj Mahal Hotel.

Donald Trump has recently become a media celebrity for his TV show, *The Apprentice*, which garnered respectable ratings in each of its 10 seasons. *The Apprentice* is a weekly elimination reality show in which 16 to 18 businesspeople contend for various upper-level positions in Trump's vast array of business ventures. NBC now pays Trump $3 million for each episode, around $40 million per season. In 2007, Trump received a star on the Hollywood Walk of Fame for his role in the show.

Though the size of his fortune is uncertain, *Forbes* has put Trump at #420 on its list of the world's richest people.

Eike Batista

Eike Batista is a Brazilian businessman and the chief executive officer of EBX Group.

Batista was born on November 3, 1956, in Governador Valadares, Brazil. His full name is Eike Fuhrken Batista da Silva. He currently lives in Rio de Janeiro.

Batista is divorced from former *Playboy* model and Carnival Queen Luma de Oliveira. They have two sons, Thor and Olin.

Batista has six brothers and sisters. Their mother was born in Hamburg, Germany; their father, Eliezer Batista da Silva, was an engineer and a highly revered Brazilian mining minister who was responsible for building a great deal of Brazil's infrastructure, including ports and railroads.

At a young age, Eike moved to Europe with his family, where Eliezer began to develop VRD (Companhia Vale do Rio Doce), now called Vale. Vale later became one of the largest mining companies in the world.

He briefly studied engineering at RWTH Aachen University but dropped out and soon returned to Brazil, where he began buying and selling gold. As his competition grew and margins decreased, Batista decided to mechanize the mine and succeeded despite his inexperience. In a 2010 *Business Week* interview with Charlie Rose, Batista admitted, "I underestimated the weather, technical conditions, diseases, logistics—but ultimately the mine was so rich, it was idiot-proof because it survived all my mistakes."

Batista then joined Canadian mining company TVX Gold, made and lost a fortune, and finally sold his interests in TVX for $1 billion, which he reinvested in mining. Eventually, Batista came to control gold mines all over the world in locations as diverse as Chile and Russia. In 2011, he took over control of Canadian gold mine company Ventana.

Batista has also invested in steel, water, and energy. He currently owns iron ore mines through the publicly traded MMX, of which he is the majority stockholder. He attracts top-flight executives by giving them equity in the company.

His holding company, EBX, is also involved in shipbuilding, entertainment, and tourism.

Much of Batista's wealth comes from his ownership of oil and gas exploration company OGX. The company was founded in 2007 and expects to begin production of oil in 2012. Batista is planning to attract foreign investors in OGX with the opening of an office in New York City in late 2011 and the listing of OGX on the London Stock Exchange.

Batista has warned against government overspending, excess borrowing, and debt.

Batista is famous for living life to the fullest, including owning and racing speedboats. As a speedboat racer, Batista won the Brazilian, world, and American championships. Although he stopped racing after the birth of his first son, he still owns a 48-foot-long Catamaran that is made of Kevlar and carbon fiber and sports two 1600 horsepower twin-supercharged V8 engines. The craft can reach speeds of over 160 miles an hour.

Batista claims to be superstitious and likes the number 63, the sun, and the letter X; these symbols are prominent in his companies' logos and names.

Batista is generous with donations. He once bid R$500,000 at an auction on a suit worn by President Lula on inauguration day, with the proceeds going to charity. Batista has also pledged an annual donation of R$20 million for five years to Rio de Janeiro's Pacifying Police Unit program.

Batista is currently the wealthiest person in Brazil, fourth richest in the Americas, and eighth richest in the world. His fortune is estimated at $27 billion. He has openly stated that he intends to become the richest person in the world.

George Kaiser

George Kaiser is president and CEO of GBK Corporation as well as the majority shareholder and chairman of the board of directors of BOK Financial Corporation. Kaiser and his wife, Myra, have three children. They split their time between homes in San Francisco, California, and Tulsa, Oklahoma.

Kaiser was born in Tulsa in 1942. He is the grandson of Jewish immigrants who fled the Nazis during World War II. Kaiser's parents and uncle founded the Kaiser-Francis Oil Company, an oil exploration and production company, in the 1940s. Kaiser attended public school in Tulsa and went on to earn a BA and MBA from Harvard.

He briefly entertained the idea of working in the Foreign Service but returned to Tulsa in 1966 to work in the family business. In 1969, Kaiser took over as head of Kaiser-Francis. He is currently the President, Chief Executive Officer (CEO), and principal owner of GBK Corporation, the parent company of Kaiser-Francis.

Kaiser bought the Bank of Oklahoma from the Federal Deposit Insurance Company (FDIC) in 1990. The FDIC is a government agency that guarantees the deposits that consumers keep in public financial institutions. By acquiring the Bank of Oklahoma, Kaiser immediately gained a spot on the *Forbes* 400 list of the wealthiest Americans.

He is also the founder of Excelerate Energy and Argonaut Private Equity.

Kaiser has a reputation as a generous philanthropist. He has established the George Kaiser Family Foundation, which helps fight childhood poverty. He is a major supporter of the Jewish community of Tulsa and has donated money to help beautify the city. Another cause supported by Kaiser is childhood education.

The Kaiser family foundation has contributed to the National Energy Policy Institute, a non-profit organization at the University of Tulsa.

In January of 2009, Kaiser drew the ire of members of the Oklahoma oil and gas industry when he testified before a committee of the state House of Representatives calling for the elimination or reduction of tax incentives for the industry and the use of the resulting revenues to provide education and health care programs for the underprivileged.

Kaiser also established the Tulsa Community Foundation. The foundation helps to organize and consolidate private donations from wealthy philanthropists to get the greatest benefit from the money. The foundation is now the largest community foundation in the United States with assets of over $4 billion.

He is one of the billionaire signers, along with Warren Buffett and Bill and Melinda Gates of the "Giving Pledge" to give away half of his fortune.

As of March, 2011, Kaiser's fortunate was estimated by *Forbes* at $9.8 billion. He is ranked as the 43rd richest person in the world.

• George Lucas

George Lucas is a screenwriter, director, and producer as well as the founder and chairman of LucasFilm, Ltd.

Lucas splits his time between homes in California and Hawaii. He is divorced from first wife, Marcia, a film editor. Lucas has three adopted children, Amanda, Katie, and Jett. He has been linked romantically to businesswoman Mellody Hobson.

Lucas was born on May 14, 1944, in Modesto, California. His father, George Lucas, Sr., ran a stationery store and owned a walnut ranch on which the family lived. His mother, Ellinore, who came from a prominent Modesto family, was an invalid for much of George's boyhood. He has three siblings.

His first love was racing cars. However, shortly before high school graduation, Lucas was involved in a serious accident, which was portrayed in his semi-autobiographical film, *American Graffiti*.

While Lucas was attending Modesto Junior College he became interested in filmmaking, going to see art films at jazz clubs and coffee bars in San Francisco. He soon entered the University of Southern California (USC) School of Cinematic Arts, one of the country's first film schools.

While at USC, Lucas made several short films, including *THX-1138*, which won an award at the 1967-68 National Student Film Festival. He also won an internship at Warner Brothers, which allowed him to meet Francis Ford Coppola, who was making *Finian's Rainbow*. Lucas and Coppola went on to form the production company American Zoetrope. Their first production was a full-length version of *THX-1138*. In 1967, Lucas graduated with a bachelor's degree in fine arts in film.

When Coppola began making *The Godfather* in 1973, Lucas decided to form his own production company, LucasFilm Ltd, in Marin County, California. The company's first film, *American Graffiti*, was a huge hit and earned Lucas five Academy Award nominations, a Golden Globe Award, and the New York Film Critics' Award.

In 1975, Lucas established Industrial Light and Magic (ILM) to help produce the special effects for *Star Wars*, which was released in 1977. Lucas waived his fees as director in exchange for a 40% stake of the profits and the licensing rights for *Star Wars*. The film turned out to be one of the most successful of all time and generated a huge personal fortune for Lucas. Lucas went on to make two sequels, *The Empire Strikes Back* and *Return of the Jedi*, and three prequels, *The Phantom Menace*, *Attack of the Clones*, and *Revenge of the Sith*, all of which were huge hits. Lifetime revenue generated by *Star Wars* amounts to $20 billion and shows no signs of stopping.

In the early 1980s Lucas teamed up with Steven Spielberg to become executive producer on the *Indiana Jones* movies, which include *Raiders of The Lost Ark*, *Indiana Jones and the Temple of Doom*, *Indiana Jones and the Last Crusade*, and *Indiana Jones and the Kingdom of the Crystal Skull*. This series also set box office records and generated huge amounts of money from licensing.

LucasFilm included a high-tech animation house named The Graphics Group that later became Pixar Studios. Lucas subsequently sold Pixar to Apple Computer's Steve Jobs for $10 million. Pixar went on to produce many computer-animated hits and Oscar-winners, including the *Toy Story* films.

Between 1980 and 1985, Lucas oversaw construction of Skywalker Ranch, a base of operations for the technical, creative, and administrative departments of LucasFilm.

He also established LucasFilm Games, later renamed LucasArts, to develop and sell computer games based on his movies.

In 1992, Lucas received the Irving G. Thalberg Award for lifetime achievement in film from the Academy of Motion Picture Arts and Sciences.

Lucas' philanthropic works include the George Lucas Educational Foundation, a non-profit foundation that encourages and awards innovation in schools. Lucas has also donated $1 million to help build the Martin Luther King Memorial on the National Mall in Washington, DC, to honor the late civil rights leader. In 2006, Lucas donated $175 million to USC to help expand the film school where he had been a student. It was the largest donation ever given to a film school as well as the largest ever to USC.

Lucas' 2011 fortune is estimated by *Forbes* at $3.2 billion.

• Gordon Moore

Gordon Moore is the co-founder and chairman emeritus of Intel Corporation.

Moore met his wife, Betty, while attending San Jose State University.

He was born on January 3, 1929, in San Francisco, California. His family lived in nearby Pescadero, where he grew up.

Moore attended San Jose State University in San Jose, California, for his freshman and sophomore years but subsequently transferred to the University of California, Berkeley, where he earned a Bachelor of Science degree in chemistry in 1950. After Berkeley, he received a PhD in chemistry with a minor in physics from the California Institute of Technology (CalTech). Moore next did post-doctoral work at Johns Hopkins Applied Physics Laboratory until 1956.

Moore and fellow CalTech graduate William Shockley joined Beckman Instruments but left with six other employees to form Fairchild Semiconductor Corporation.

In July of 1968, Moore co-founded Intel Corporation with Bob Noyce. Moore first served as executive vice president and then president in 1975. In April of 1979, Moore was named chairman of the board and chief executive officer. He was named chairman emeritus in 1997.

As a pioneer in the semiconductor industry, Moore's contributions to technology include the development of integrated-circuit processing, MOS memory, and the microprocessor computer.

Moore is also famous for being the author of Moore's Law, which was published in an article in *Electronics Magazine* on April 19, 1965. In the article, written while he was a 36-year-old researcher working at a Palo Alto semiconductor lab, Moore predicted that the number of components, including transistors, that could fit onto one silicon microchip would double each year (the claim was later revised to every 18 to 24 months), over time increasing their processing power while lowering their prices exponentially. At the time, the prediction seemed outrageous, but over time it proved accurate that Moore's Law has migrated from obscure techie rule of thumb to becoming a cornerstone of pop culture. Moore's Law has been used in reference to everything from presidential elections to cardiovascular research.

Moore served as a member of the Business Advisory Board of Gilead Sciences from 1991 until 1996, when he became a member of the board of directors.

Moore is also a former chairman and current life trustee of CalTech, a member of the National Academy of Engineering, and a Fellow of the UK's Royal Society of Engineering.

Moore and his wife have established the Gordon and Betty Moore Foundation. The foundation's philanthropic efforts focus on education and technology. In 2001, the Moores gave $600 million to Caltech, the largest gift ever made to an institution of higher education. The Moore Laboratories building at CalTech and the library at the Centre for Mathematical Sciences at the University of Cambridge are both named after Moore. In 2007, the Moores donated $200 million towards the construction of the world's largest optical telescope at Caltech and the University of California.

Among the many honors Moore has received are the Bower Award for Business Leadership and the 2008 IEEE Medal of Honor. In 2003, he was elected a Fellow of the American Association for the Advancement of Science. More has also received the National Medal of Technology and the Presidential Medal of Freedom, the United States' highest civilian honor.

In 2011, Moore's was the first human genome sequenced on Ion Torrent's Personal Genome Machine platform sequencing device.

In his spare time, Moore enjoys hobbies such as painting cars and building model airplanes. He is an avid fisherman and a conservationist.

His 2011 estimated wealth of $4 billion places him at 268th on the *Forbes* list.

Harold Hamm

Harold Hamm is the CEO and a director of Continental Resources, an oil and gas exploration and production company. He lives in Enid, Oklahoma, with his wife Sue Ann, who works with him in both his business and philanthropic pursuits. The couple has five children.

Hamm was born December 11, 1945, the youngest of 13 children of Oklahoma sharecroppers. While growing up in a one-bedroom house, he worked at as many odd jobs as he could find in order to help his parents with expenses, including fixing cars, milking cows, pumping gas, and working in a lumber yard.

Hamm graduated from Enid High School. In 1965, after an oil boom hit near his hometown, he borrowed $1,000 to buy a truck and began hauling water and drilling mud to the oilrigs. He formed the Shelly Dean Oil Company, which later became Continental Resources, in 1967. When Hamm's first big strike came in 1971, he was a 26-year-old wildcat driller.

Today Hamm owns more gas and oil than any other American. His reserves in the Bakken, an area in western North Dakota, are estimated at well over 8 billion barrels.

Hamm is also the chairman of the board of directors of Hiland Partners, LP, a publicly owned natural gas processing and gathering company and of Hiland Holdings GP, LP, which is also a public company traded on the NASDAQ. Hiland Holdings owns the general partner interest in Hiland Partners LP. He is also a director of Complete Production Services, Inc., a public oil and gas service company whose shares are traded on the New York Stock Exchange (NYSE).

Positions formerly held by Hamm include chairman of the Oklahoma Independent Petroleum Association, founder and chairman of Save Domestic Oil, Inc., as well as co-founder and chairman of the Oklahoma Energy Resources Board. Additionally, he has held the position of president of the National Stripper Well Association and co-founded the Domestic Energy Producers Alliance.

Sue Ann Hamm is an integral part of Harold's companies and philanthropic endeavors. She is a member of the Oklahoma Bar Association, works as Marketing Manager at Continental Resources, and serves as secretary of the executive board of the Oklahoma Energy Resources Board, which promotes the education of future oil industry employees. She is also a past chairman of the board of the Crude Oil Committee of the Oklahoma Independent Petroleum Association.

After Harold was diagnosed with diabetes, he and Sue Ann began contributing millions of dollars to diabetes research and education, including a $7 million pledge to the Oklahoma Diabetes Center at the University of Oklahoma Health Sciences Center and a $3 million donation to acquire the building that later became the Harold Hamm Oklahoma Diabetes Center, as well as $2 million to the Oklahoma Diabetes Center and an additional $1.4 million to fund research and clinical activities.

The Hamms also show their support for higher education with contributions to the University of North Dakota School of Engineering and Mines. In addition, they have endowed three faculty chairs at Oklahoma University: one in clinical diabetes research, one in adult diabetes, and one in adult diabetes clinical care or research. They also support the Cancer Institute Satellite Facility on OU's Tulsa campus.

Harold Hamm has been awarded honorary degrees by the University of Oklahoma and Northwestern Oklahoma State University.

Forbes ranks Hamm as the 33rd richest person in the U.S., with a net worth estimated at $8.6 billion.

• Henry Ross Perot

Henry Ross Perot, more commonly known as Ross Perot, is widely known for his presidential candidacies in 1992 and 1996. He is also an extremely wealthy businessman. Forbes.com has listed him as the 232nd wealthiest person in the world as of March 2011, with his net worth estimated to be $3.4 billion.

Perot is a Texas native, born on June 27, 1930. He remains married to Margot, his wife of 53 years. The two have five children together, and numerous grandchildren.

After joining the Boy Scouts of America in 1941, Perot reached the rank of Eagle Scout in less than thirteen months, an extraordinary feat. He has also been honored with the Distinguished Eagle Scout Award, an honor given to those who demonstrate exceptional professional and community service for a minimum of 25 years after achieving the rank of Eagle Scout.

In 1949, Perot joined the US Naval Academy, and in 1953 he graduated as battalion commander and class president. He later admitted his dissatisfaction with Navy life in a letter to his father. Shortly after he resigned his Navy commission he married Margot Birmingham.

In 1957 he began working for IBM, almost immediately becoming one of the company's top salesmen. He wanted to become more involved in the company, sharing his thoughts with superiors who ignored his ideas. In 1962, he left the company in order to start his own, Electronic Data Systems (EDS), which focused on data processing. One of the first substantial contracts awarded to the company was the computerization of all Medicare records.

In 1968 he took EDS public, initially releasing shares at a price of $16 each. Within a few days the price per EDS share had gone up tenfold to $160. Perot remained the primary owner of EDS until General Motors purchased a controlling share of the company for $2.4 billion in 1984.

In 1988 he started Perot Systems Corporations, Inc., and was the CEO until he handed the position over to his son, Ross Perot, Jr. Perot systems was an information technology service focusing on industries such as government and healthcare records. Dell Inc. acquired the company in September 2009 for $3.9 billion.

In 1992 he started his first bid for the United States presidency, running as an independent, saying that he would run for president if his supporters could get his name on the ballot of all fifty states. He benefited from a lull in the campaigns of the Democratic and Republican Presidential nominees that occurred after their intraparty campaign victories. During that time there was a large, widely publicized effort by his supporters to have his name included on the election ballot of all fifty states. By the summer of 1992, Perot garnered a commanding lead in preliminary polls, but votes slowly trickled to other candidates. The decline in popularity is largely attributed to his lack of cooperation with his campaign managers, since he frequently ignored their advice.

Perot continued to lose popularity until he finally announced on Larry King Live that he would not seek the presidency. He later stated that the real reason behind dropping out of the race was that the Bush campaign threatened to release lewd photos of his daughter that had been digitally altered. Perot stated that he wished to protect his daughter from humiliation and did not want the controversy to affect her wedding plans.

Despite his withdrawal, he qualified for all fifty state ballots. He told his daughter of the scandal after her marriage. She urged him to continue his bid for the presidency, which he did. At that time, he publicized the reason he had dropped out, though many doubted him. It was later confirmed that the hoax had been set up by supporters of GOP candidate George H.W. Bush and that no such pictures existed.

Perot managed to acquire 18.6% of the popular vote in the 1992 election, but that translated to zero electoral votes. His was the most successful bid for the presidency by a third-party candidate since Theodore Roosevelt ran for the Progressive Party in the 1912 election.

In 1995 Perot founded the Reform Party, and in 1996, he ran for presidency again, but drew only 8% of the popular vote in his second bid for office. Since then, he has remained largely uninvolved with politics, even refusing to answer simple political questions in some cases.

• James Goodnight

James Goodnight is a co-founder and chief executive officer (CEO) of computing giant SAS Institute.

Goodnight was born on January 6, 1943, in Salisbury, North Carolina. His family subsequently moved to Greensboro and then on to Wilmington when James was 12 years old. James' parents, Albert and Dorothy Patterson Goodnight, are both deceased. His father owned a hardware store in Wilmington where James often worked.

As a student at New Hanover High School, Goodnight's best subjects were chemistry and math. Goodnight attended North Carolina State University in Raleigh where, during his sophomore year, he fell in love with computers and computer science. It was at NC State that Goodnight met and became close friends with Bruce Griffith who, along with help from technology developed by Goodnight, went on to make a fortune in the forestry and private equity businesses.

The summer between his sophomore and junior years, Goodnight got a job as a programmer for the NC State agricultural economics department. During his senior year at NC State, he met his future wife, Ann, who was a student at Meredith College. While at NC State, Goodnight joined the Tau Kappa Epsilon fraternity. After he earned his fortune, he contributed towards the building of a brand-new TKE fraternity house at NC State.

After earning his bachelor's degree, Goodnight attended graduate school at NC State. During his master's degree studies, he became intrigued by the Apollo program and the possibility of humans one day walking on the moon. He was able to get hired for a programmer position at a company that was making communications equipment for Apollo ground stations.

Goodnight later went on to earn his PhD in Statistics from NC State and taught there from 1972 to 1976. In 1976, Goodnight co-founded Statistical Analysis System, or SAS, along with Anthony Bar, John Sall, and Jane Helwig.

SAS's original product was a package of statistical analysis modules that ran on IBM mainframes. SAS's innovation was the ability to code and test programs in windows instead of having to write them, submit them in batch mode, and wait for the results to be returned.

As other brands of computers became more powerful and sophisticated, SAS adapted its software to those platforms, porting its user interface to the new machines. In this way, SAS users were able to easily move among systems. Eventually even desktop PCs became powerful enough that SAS could run on them.

SAS's business intelligence and customer relationship management software remains the standard for submitting statistics of clinical pharmaceutical trials to the Food and Drug Administration. Other uses of SAS's software include statistical analysis in the insurance industry as well as data mining, entry, and warehousing.

As Microsoft's Windows Operating System became more popular, challenges arose for SAS. For one thing, SAS continued to charge yearly licensing fees rather than allowing customers to purchase the software. Another challenge was adapting SAS's user interface to be compatible with Windows. SAS managed to overcome these obstacles and continued to expand.

Today SAS is one of the largest privately-held companies in North Carolina and the software business, with nearly 12,000 employees and annual earnings of $2.4 billion. A full quarter of its annual revenue is returned to the company to fund research and development.

SAS has been ranked the #1 place to work in the United States by *Fortune* magazine, with employees enjoying perks such as fully stocked break rooms and a fitness center.

Goodnight is very interested in supporting education, especially for elementary and high school students. He is a major contributor to the Cary Academy, a private school in North Carolina located near the SAS site. The company has also sponsored the new mathematics building at NC State, named SAS Hall.

Goodnight is also the owner of the Prestonwood Country Club in Cary, NC, and its famous Red Fox restaurant.

Forbes estimates Goodnight's current wealth at $6.9 billion.

James Jannard

James "Jim" Jannard is the founder and former chairman of the board of directors of Oakley, known for its trendy eye wear, apparel, and sporting goods. Oakley is a manufacturer based in Foothill Ranch, California. Jannard is also an avid photographer who founded the RED Digital Cinema Camera Company, a manufacturer of ultra-high-resolution video cameras that are used in many high-end Hollywood film productions.

Jannard and his wife live in the San Juan Islands region of Washington State. They own homes on Orcas Island as well as on their personal islands of Spieden, Washington, and the Fijian Islands of Kaibu and Vatu Vara Islands. The couple has four children and twelve grandchildren.

Jannard was born in 1949 and grew up in Alhambra, California. He attended pharmacy school at the University of Southern California (USC), located in Los Angeles, but dropped out during his junior year.

In 1975, Jannard founded Oakley with $300, naming it after his dog Oakley Anne, an English setter. He served as chairman of the board of directors as well as CEO and, later, president, before eventually selling his interests in the company.

Oakley's first product was a handgrip for BMX cross-country bicycles and motorcycles. The company entered the high-end eyewear business in 1980 with the introduction of the Oakley O/20 Goggle. In 1984, Jannard designed the Oakley Eyeshade sunglasses. Nine years later, in 1992, Oakley passed RayBan to become the most popular brand of sunglasses in the world.

Rather than imitating its competitors by hiring famous sports stars to endorse its products, Oakley built its reputation by concentrating on its ability to innovate and a nose for style and fashion. Its products were soon embraced by surfers and skiers. The company developed and produced high-tech products such as glasses with polycarbonate lenses that can withstand shotgun blasts, fire-resistant clothing, as well as sunglasses equipped with mp3 players and wireless Bluetooth devices.

In 1995, the company went public on the New York Stock Exchange (NYSE). Jannard eventually sold his interests in Oakley to Italian high-fashion luxury eye wear conglomerate Luxottica s.P.a. for $2.2 billion in 2007.

Jannard founded RED Digital Cinema in 2005. A prototype of the company's first camera, the RED ONE, was introduced in 2006 at the National Association of Broadcasters (NAB) convention in Las Vegas, Nevada. The company made its first shipments of the RED ONE in 2007 at a cost of about $30,000 for a complete package.

The RED ONE is a 4K digital video camera, which means that the video is shot at 4,000 lines, much higher than the 1,080 of High Definition (HD) cameras. RED also sells a 3K version, dubbed Scarlet, for between $3,000 and $15,000, as well as a 5K camera named EPIC.

The RED ONE has been supported and adopted by director Steven Soderbergh and Academy Award winning film maker Peter Jackson. It has been used in the production of such films as *Pirates of the Caribbean: On Stranger Tides*, *The Social Network*, and *The Hobbit*.

Jannard, who holds over 600 patents, was named one of the 100 most creative people in the world by *Fast Company* magazine.

He is an avid photographer and maintains a website of his photographs. For the first twenty years of Oakley's existence, Jannard shot all of its ads and commercials.

Oakley and RED Digital have both sponsored racecars.

Jannard has owned four jet airplanes: a Falcon 20, a Falcon 50, and two Global Express jets, including his current Bombardier.

In 2010, *Forbes* magazine ranked Jannard 376th on its list of the world's richest people, with an estimated net worth of $3.0 billion.

James Kennedy

James Kennedy is the chairman of the board of directors and chief executive officer (CEO) of communications giant, Cox Enterprises.

Kennedy lives in Atlanta, Georgia, with his wife, Sarah. They have three children. Kennedy was born in Honolulu, Hawaii, in 1949. He is the grandson of James M. Cox, the founder of Cox Enterprises, who began his career as a newspaper editor and owner before entering politics. Cox served as three-time governor of Ohio and was a presidential candidate in 1920. Cox passed away in 1957.

In 1970, Kennedy graduated from the University of Denver (DU) with a bachelor's degree in business administration.

He began working for Cox Enterprises in Atlanta, Georgia, in 1972, learning the business from the ground up. He first worked for Cox Newspapers, where he held a variety of jobs such as production assistant, copy editor, reporter, business manager, ad salesman, and executive vice president and general manager.

In 1979 he moved to Grand Junction, Colorado, where he served as president of Grand Junction Newspapers, Inc, and soon became publisher of the Grand Junction Daily Sentinel.

Kennedy then returned to Atlanta, where he became vice president of Cox Newspapers, a subsidiary of Cox Enterprises. The following year he was named executive vice president of Cox Enterprises and, in January 1988, he became chairman and CEO.

When Kennedy's mother, Barbara Cox Anthony, died in 2007, he inherited 25% of the company.

Under Kennedy's direction, Cox Enterprises' annual revenue increased from $1.8 billion to $15 billion. Today, the company is ranked among the top 10 in the nation in every area of operations. Holdings include the Cox Communications cable company, 86 radio stations, 17 newspapers, 15 television stations, Manheim car auctions, and AutoTrader.com.

He was awarded an honorary doctorate of humane letters from Kennesaw State University in Georgia in 2003 and inducted into the J. Mack Robinson College of Business Hall of Fame at Georgia State University the following year.

James and his wife Sarah have been honored for their philanthropic work with several organizations and, in 2003, the couple received the Philanthropists of the Year award from the Greater Atlanta Chapter of the Association for Fund-raising Professionals.

Kennedy is an environmentalist and avid outdoorsman who has given his support to many conservation initiatives and causes. He served as chairman of the Colorado Division of Wildlife Commission while working at the Sentinel and received the Conservationist of the Year award.

Additionally, Kennedy has served as president of Wetlands America Trust, Inc., as well as the Chairman of the Colorado Division of Wildlife Commission. He currently serves on the board of directors of the Ducks Unlimited Atlanta Committee for Progress and is a director of the PATH Foundation, a non-profit organization that builds networks of scenic trails in Georgia for cyclists, skaters, and pedestrians.

In 2008, he established the James C. Kennedy Endowed Chair in Waterfowl and Wetlands Conservation at Mississippi State University's Department of Wildlife & Fisheries of the College of Forest Resources. His donation sustains a teaching, research, and outreach program in waterfowl and wetlands ecology and conservation at MSU in perpetuity.

Kennedy has also made generous donations of both money and time to the University of Denver. He has served as a member of DU's Board of Trustees and created the James C. Kennedy Institute for Educational Success in the Morgridge College of Education with a $10 million gift to the school. The purpose of the Kennedy Institute is to help underprivileged children succeed in education.

Kennedy also had a great deal of success as a competitive cyclist, earning National, Pan-American, and World Championship titles in the 3,000-meter pursuit. In 1992 he was captain of the world-record team that won the Race Across America. Kennedy was also one of five cyclists elected to the United States Cycling Federation Master's All-American team and for three years served as honorary chairman of the Bike Tours of the National Multiple Sclerosis Society's Georgia Chapter. In 1997, he served as honorary chairman of the American Diabetes Association's Tour de Cure.

Kennedy's current net worth is estimated at $6.2 billion, which places him at 49th in the United States and 154th in the world.

Jeff Bezos

Jeff Bezos is the founder and CEO of online retailer amazon.com.

He currently lives in Seattle, Washington, with his wife, Mackenzie. They have four children.

He was born in Albuquerque, New Mexico, on January 12, 1964. His birth name was Jeffrey Preston Jorgensen. His parents were Jacklyn Gise Jorgensen and Ted Jorgensen. Jacklyn was a teenager, and the marriage lasted only a year.

When Jeff was five, Jacklyn remarried. Miguel "Mike" Bezos was a native of Cuba who had come to U.S. by himself at the age of 15. After Miguel graduated from the University of Albuquerque he married Jacklyn and legally adopted Jeff. The family then moved to Houston, Texas, where Miguel worked as an engineer at Exxon.

Jeff's maternal grandfather was a regional director of the Atomic Energy Commission. His grandparents also owned a 25,000-acre ranch. After his grandfather took early retirement, Jeff spent his summers working alongside his grandfather at the ranch.

From the beginning, Bezos displayed an aptitude for science and mechanics. Stories about his early years include his attempt to disassemble his crib with a screwdriver, rigging an alarm system to keep his siblings out of his room, and converting the family garage into a science lab.

The family next moved to Miami, where Bezos attended Miami Palmetto Senior High School. While in high school, Jeff also attended the Student Science Training Program at the University of Florida. He was an excellent student – the valedictorian of his class.

After graduation, he attended Princeton University. His first major was physics but he switched to engineering and computer science. Bezos graduated summa cum laude in 1986 with a Bachelor of Science degree. He was a member of the prestigious Phi Beta Kappa academic honor society.

Bezos had a brief stint working on Wall Street in computers and building computer networks. He also worked as a financial analyst at D. E. Shaw & Co and was a vice president of Bankers Trust. It was while he was at Shaw that Jeff met his future wife, Mackenzie, who was also a Princeton graduate.

One day in the spring of 1994, Bezos realized that Internet usage was growing by 2,300% per year and decided it presented a great opportunity for buying and selling products. Bezos looked at the top twenty mail order businesses and decided that books were the ideal commodity for sale over the Internet, because there was no comprehensive mail order catalogue and the Internet was the perfect place to house a huge database that could reach an unlimited number of customers.

The next day Bezos flew to Los Angeles, where he attended the American Booksellers' Convention in order to learn the book business. When he realized that the major book wholesalers already had computerized lists, he decided to start his own business. He chose Seattle because it was close to book wholesaler Ingram and there was a steady supply of computer talent.

On July 4, 1994, Jeff and Mackenize flew to Texas, where they collected a 1988 Chevy Blazer from Mike Bezos.

Mackenzie drove while Jeff created a business plan. They named the company Amazon after the South American river with its many tributaries.

The couple arrived in Seattle and set up the company in their garage. As soon as the site was ready, Jeff got their friends and acquaintances to test it. All went well, and the site went live on July 16, 1995. With only word-of-mouth advertising, within 30 days Amazon had sold books in 50 states and 45 countries. By late summer, its sales had reached $20,000 a week.

In 1997 the company went public and Bezos and the original investors soon became millionaires.

The company continued to diversify its merchandise and expand into areas such as CDs, DVDs, electronics, toys, and more. Amazon is now the world's largest online retailer of any kind and is aiming to increase its market share by going head-to-head with Netflix with its new movie streaming service, Amazon Prime.

Even when the dotcom bubble burst, Amazon's profits continued to increase, because it emphasized customer service and its Six Core Values of customer obsession, ownership, bias for action, frugality, high hiring bar and innovation.

One of Amazon's greatest successes came with the Kindle electronic book reader. The company is now taking on the iPad by selling the Kindle 3G in AT&T stores.

Bezos has also launched a human spaceflight company in Texas named Blue Origin whose goal is to build reusable rocket ships and encourage space tourism. The company is currently building a vertical-takeoff, vertical-landing rocket ship.

In 1999, *Time* magazine named Bezos its Person of the Year. In 2008, *U.S. News & World Report* listed Bezos as one of America's Best Leaders and Carnegie Mellon University awarded him an honorary doctorate in Science and Technology.

Despite worries about Amazon after the recent demise of Borders, the company continues to grow at an annual rate of more than 50%.

Bezos takes a minimum salary as CEO and declines stock options, but he owns 20% of Amazon's stock. He has a reputation as a micro-manager who pays strict attention to the details of the business but is at the same time charming and lighthearted.

With a 2011 net worth of $18.1 billion, Bezos is ranked by *Forbes* as #14 in the U.S. and #30 in the world.

• John Franklyn Mars

John Franklyn Mars is the chairman of the board of directors of giant food and confection conglomerate Mars, Incorporated.

Mars and his wife, Adrienne, whom he married in 1958, recently moved from Arlington, Virginia, to Jackson, Wyoming, upon John's retirement. They have three children: Linda Anne, Frank Edward, and Michael John.

John Mars was born on October 15, 1935. He is the grandson of the founders of Mars, Frank and Ethel Mars, who began making chocolates in their small kitchen in Tacoma, Washington, in 1919.

James' father, Forrest Mars, Sr., took over the business and continued the family confection-making tradition, inventing M&Ms and introducing the malt-flavored nougat used in the centers of Mars' famous candy bars, including Milky Way, Three Musketeers, and Snickers.

John attended and graduated from Yale University with a Bachelor of Arts and Science degree.

Upon the death of their father in 1999, John and his brother, Forrest Mars, Jr., and sister, Jacqueline Mars, inherited the company.

The company, which is headquartered in McLean, Virginia, employs more than 65,000 associates at over 370 sites, including 135 factories in approximately 68 countries worldwide. The company has organized its operations into six separate divisions, including Chocolate, Pet Care, Wrigley's Gum and Confections, Food, Drinks, and Symbioscience.

The Mars chocolate line now includes Twix, M&Ms, Three Musketeers, and Skittles. The company also operates Ethel's Chocolate Lounges, a group of Chicago-area boutiques that allow customers to sample components of the new Ethel chocolate line.

In October of 2009, Mars acquired chewing gum giant Wm. Wrigley Jr. Co. for $23 billion. The merger created world's largest confectionery company, with combined annual sales estimated at between $22 and $28 billion. The Wrigley line includes Xtra, Orbit, Doublemint, Skittles, Starburst, Altoids, Juicy Fruit, Freedent, Airwaves, Life Savers, Eclipse, and Winterfresh, just to name a few.

Other lines include Uncle Ben's Rice, as well as electronic components for vending machines.

Mars' growing pet food division produces Whiskas and Pedigree pet foods. It recently bought Doane Pet Care, the makers of Wal-Mart's Ol' Roy label, and the maker of Greenies, the country's top-selling dog treat.

The Symbioscience division produces Cirkuhealth, Wisdom Panel, Mx, Seramis, and Mycocoapaper.

John Mars is also a key employee of Mars Horsecare UK, Limited, formerly Effem Equine, a regional corporate brand of Mars and producer of United Kingdom equestrian feed brands such as Spillers, Winergy, Equivite, and Buckeye.

Mars has a corporate initiative of consolidating its products under a single corporate brand name in order to leverage the credibility and goodwill that the company has earned through its world-famous product brands.

The initiative is also designed to reduce complexity, provide a single point of reference, and build greater awareness for the business.

John Mars is reportedly focused on and obsessed with punctuality, efficiency, and quantitative measurement of quality in all of the Mars factories. This is evident in the company's touted "Five Principles" which are listed on the company's web site as follows:

"Quality: The consumer is our boss, quality is our work and value for money is our goal.

"Responsibility: As individuals, we demand total responsibility from ourselves; as Associates, we support the responsibilities of others.

"Mutuality: A mutual benefit is a shared benefit; a shared benefit will endure.

"Efficiency: We use resources to the full, waste nothing and do only what we can do best.

"Freedom: We need freedom to shape our future; we need profit to remain free. Quality, Responsibility, Mutuality, Efficiency and Freedom."

John Mars has a reputation for being extremely private and reclusive. Not even *Forbes* could find a photograph of him to run when they published their 2010 list of the world's richest people.

Mars' fortune is currently estimated at $10 billion. He is tied for 81st place on the *Forbes* ranking of the richest people in the world.

• John Menard

John R. Menard is the founder and owner of the Menard's home improvement store chain.

He lives in Eau Claire, Wisconsin. Menard is divorced and has six children. Born in 1940, he is the oldest of eight children of Rosemary and John Menard, Sr., who instilled in their children their values of hard work, frugality, and independence.

Menard began learning the construction business from his father when he worked his way through college. He spent summers during his college years as a handyman constructing post-frame buildings to finance his education. After only two years, while he was still in his twenties, Menard hired his own crew to provide pole buildings.

John attended a Catholic high school and, in 1963, he received his bachelor's degree from the University of Wisconsin at Eau Claire.

He opened his first hardware store in 1972. Menard's is now the third-largest home improvement chain in the country, behind only Home Depot and Lowe's. The chain has 286 stores in 13 states throughout the Midwest and employs more than 37,000 workers. It has estimated annual gross sales of $5.5 billion. Menard's stores differentiate themselves from their competitors by featuring full-service lumberyards.

The housing crash and subsequent recession have actually helped Menard's, as people began making do-it-yourself repairs and upgrades to their homes rather than selling their houses and moving.

Since 2001, John Menard has been involved with Polaris Industries Inc. as a member of the board of directors, the Corporate Governance & Nominating Committee, and the Technology Committee.

Menard is notorious for his hard-line business practices and has a reputation as a union buster. He has been investigated by the AFL-CIO for illegal and unfair labor practices.

A racing aficionado, for over 30 years Menard has owned and sponsored Indycar racing teams including his Team Menard. More recently, he became a partner in the #27 NASCAR Robby Gordon Motorsports team. Menard is the father of NASCAR driver Paul Menard, who won the Brickyard 400 in 2010.

Menard also owns a thoroughbred horse-breeding farm in Kentucky and is the owner of several racehorses, including aspiring Kentucky Derby entrants.

Menard has contributed money to political causes and parties, with the great majority of his donations going to Republican candidates. More recently he has also donated to Independent candidates.

In January of 2008, Menard gave $15 million to Luther Midelfort Hospital in Eau Claire. The money was earmarked to be used toward building a new emergency department at the hospital. He has also established the Mayo Clinic's Menard Transformational Fund for Education to help the Mayo Clinic train and educate doctors and other health care professionals.

As of March 2011, Menard's fortune was estimated by *Forbes* at $5.2 billion. He is the richest person in Wisconsin.

• John Paulson

John Paulson is the founder and president of Paulson & Co., a New York City-based hedge fund.

Paulson resides in the Upper East Side of New York City with his wife, Jenny, and their two daughters. The family also owns homes in Southampton, New York, and Aspen, Colorado.

Paulson was born on December 14, 1955, in Queens, New York. His father, Alfredo Paulson, was the chief financial officer of Ruder Finn.

Paulson attended the Whitestone Hebrew Centre school in Whitestone, New York. He earned a Bachelor of Science degree in finance from the Leonard N. Stern School of Business at New York University's College of Business and Public Administration, where he graduated first in his class, and an MBA from Harvard Business School.

Paulson began his career working at the Boston Consulting Group. He subsequently joined Odyssey Partners with Leon Levy. He then got a position in the mergers and acquisitions department at Bear Stearns. He next became a partner at arbitrage firm Gruss Partners, LP.

In 1994, Paulson founded his own hedge fund, Paulson & Co., with $2 million. Hedge funds are privately managed investment funds that use advanced strategies to offset losses during stock market downturns. These funds generate higher returns than traditional stocks and bonds. Paulson's best-known portfolios are the Advantage and Advantage Plus funds. Other funds include the Paulson Partners fund and the Credit Opportunities fund.

In 2007 Paulson earned billions of dollars betting against the subprime mortgage market.

In 2008, Paulson started a new fund that loaned money to investment banks and hedge funds during the mortgage crisis.

Paulson co-wrote a Wall Street Journal article in 2008 that suggested an alternative to the Treasury Secretary's plan for stabilizing the markets.

In 2011, Paulson & Co. managed assets of about $35 billion.

Not all of Paulson's business deals have been successful. The downturn of the stock market in 2011 caused his fund's holdings to drop from $19 billion in March to $16 billion in August. Additionally, he lost almost $500 million on an investment in Chinese lumber company Sino-Forest, whose shares dropped precipitously when the company was accused of fraud.

Paulson has made $140,000 worth of political contributions since 2000. About 45% of these contributions went to Republicans, 16% to Democrats, and 36% to special interests.

Paulson's philanthropic contributions between 2009 and 2011 included charitable donations of $20 million to the New York University Stern School of Business; $15 million to build a children's hospital in Guayaquil, Ecuador; an additional $15 million to the Center for Responsible Lending; and £2.5 million for the John A.

Paulson Chair in European Political Economy at the London School of Economics.

Paulson was ranked 39th on the 2011 *Forbes* list of the world's wealthiest people, with a net worth of nearly $16 billion.

Karl Albrecht

Karl Albrecht is a German entrepreneur. He co-founded the discount supermarket chain, Aldi (a combination of Albrecht and Discount), with his late brother, Theo.

Albrecht is married and the father of two children, neither of who works in the family business.

Karl Albrecht was born in Essen, Germany, on January 20, 1920. His father was a miner who later became a baker, while his mother owned a small grocery store in the working district of Essen. In their early days, Karl's younger brother, Theo, apprenticed at the family grocery store, while Karl apprenticed at a delicatessen.

During World War II, Albrecht served in the German army.

After the war in 1946, the brothers took over their mother's small grocery store. By 1955 they had 100 Aldi stores and by 1960 that number grew to over 300. In 1960 the two brothers split the company into Aldi Nord (North) and Aldi Sud (South). Karl took charge of the area south of Ruhr as well as the rights to the brand in the United States, the United Kingdom, and Australia. Theo took over the northern area and the rights in the rest of Europe.

By 1997, the chain had grown into one of the largest discount supermarkets in the world. The brothers controlled over 3,000 German stores and many more in other countries. Aldi has since grown even more, and the brothers now own over 8,500 stores, including over 1,000 in the United States alone. Aldi's latest store was opened in New York City in late 2010. Annual sales of the grocery chain are currently estimated at more than $67 billion.

In 1994, Karl Albrecht retired from the daily operations of Aldi Süd and became the Chairman of the Board of Directors. In 2002, he also stepped down from that position and gave up control of the firm. Today, Albrecht is retired and the Aldi stores are no longer run by any of Karl Albrecht's family members.

The extremely reclusive and intensely private Albrecht reportedly lives in Mulheim an der Ruhr, Germany. Now completely retired, he is known to enjoy raising orchids and collecting antique typewriters. He is also an avid golfing fan and built his own golf course, the Öschberghof, in 1976.

Albrecht's 2011 wealth is estimated at $25.5 million. He is the wealthiest person in Germany and the 12th richest, and oldest, person on *Forbes*' list of the wealthiest people in the world.

• Lakshmi Mittal

Lakshmi Mittal is the Indian-born chairman of the board of directors and chief executive officer (CEO) of ArcelorMittal, the world's largest steelmaker.

He is a citizen of India but lives in London with his wife, Usha. They have two children, Vanisha and Aditya. Vanisha's wedding holds the record as the most expensive in history.

Mittal was born on June 15, 1950, in Sadulpur, Rajasthan, India. His family subsequently moved to Calcutta. He earned his bachelor of commerce degree in business and accounting from St. Xavier's College in Calcutta.

In the 1970s, Mittal began working at the family steel business, Nippon Denro Ispat, whose main assets were a steel factory and a cold-rolling mill for sheet steel. In 1976, Mittal established the company's international division, starting with a dilapidated plant in Indonesia.

Due to differences of opinion within the family, Mittal left the family business in 1994. When he struck out on his own, Mittal began by buying struggling steel mills in Eastern Europe at low prices. He pioneered the use of direct reduced iron (DRI) as a scrap metal substitute and developed integrated mini-mills. Today Mittal Steel operates plants in 14 different countries.

Mittal's business operations have not been without controversy.

In 1999, Mittal purchased the Irish Steel plant based in Cork from the government for £1 million. Three years later he closed it, leaving 400 unemployed workers and an environmental mess. The government unsuccessfully sued Mittal for the anticipated €70 million costs to clean up Cork Harbour.

In 2002, Mittal was involved in an influence-peddling scheme dubbed "Garbagegate" and "the Mittal Affair". Mittal's LNM steel company sought British Prime Minister Tony Blair's help to buy Romania's state steel industry. A letter from Blair to the Romanian government hinted that the sale to Mittal might grease the wheels for Romania's entry into the European Union.

Mittal has been accused of safety violations at his Kazakhstan coalmines. In 2004, 23 miners died in explosions caused by faulty gas detectors. Between 2004 and 2007, a total of 91 deaths caused by lax standards were the subject of a criminal investigation. Witnesses to a 2006 explosion that claimed the lives of 41 people claimed that the mine's managers forced employees to work to meet production targets despite plumes of flammable gas. ArcelorMittal now has a "CSR" program intended to produce safe sustainable steel.

Mittal recently sold his shares in his Kazakhstan refinery for $1.1 billion.

Mittal is currently a member of the boards of directors of Goldman Sachs and of European Aeronautic Defense and Space Company (EADS). He belongs to the Executive Committee of the World Steel Association, the Investors' Council to the Cabinet of Ministers of Ukraine, the Foreign Investment Council in Kazakhstan, the International Investment Council in South Africa, and the Business Council of the World Economic Forum, as well as the Presidential International Advisory Board of Mozambique and the Executive Committee of the International Iron and Steel Institute. Mittal also owns Karrick, Limited.

Mittal also serves as a board council member of the Prime Minister of India's Global Advisory Council of Overseas Indians and is a member of the advisory board of the Kellogg School of Management, the Executive Board at the Indian School of Business, and the London chapter of the alumni association of St. Xavier's College.

The Lakshmi Niwas Mittal and Usha Mittal Foundation has joined with the Government of Rajasthan to establish the LNM Institute of Information Technology (LNMIIT), a non-profit organization that focuses on research.

A soccer fan, Mittal is part owner of the British team, the Queens Park Rangers.

Mittal's philanthropic pursuits include The ArcelorMittal Foundation, which supports projects in the countries in which ArcelorMittal operates. He also donated approximately £1 million to Comic Relief.

Mittal has also established the Mittal Champions Trust, contributing $9 million to support 10 Indian Olympic athletes. After shooter Abhinav Bindra won India's first-ever Olympic gold medal in 2008, Mittal awarded her 15 million rupees (about $328,000). Mittal recently donated the funds to build a 400-foot sculpture for London's Olympic Park that is scheduled to be completed in time for the 2012 Olympic Games.

Mittal lives in a 12-bedroom mansion in London's posh Kensington neighborhood. He recently purchased Alderbrook Park in Surrey, where he is building a zero-carbon-footprint estate. He paid £5.25 million for the property and is planning to spend £25 million to make it 100% self-sufficient and eco-friendly.

With a fortune estimated by *Forbes* at $31.1 billion, Mittal is the richest person in the United Kingdom, second richest in Europe, and sixth-richest in the world.

• Larry Ellison

Lawrence Joseph Ellison, commonly known as Larry Ellison, is the co-founder and CEO of software giant Oracle Corporation. He is one of the wealthiest individuals to come out of Silicon Valley. He is a philanthropist, although he is very quiet about it, considering the donations a very personal matter. Over the years he has donated hundreds of millions of dollars to medical research and education, and plans to give billions more before he dies. He has also publicly stated that he will allocate at least 95% of his estate to charitable causes. He is one of 40 billionaires to sign *The Giving Pledge*, a pledge created by Bill Gates and Warren Buffett to encourage the extremely wealthy to commit a large portion of their assets to charitable causes.

He has been married and divorced four times and has two children.

Ellison has a penchant for exotic cars. He is the owner of many, including a McLaren F1, a Lexus LFA, and an Audi R8. His personal favorite is the Acura NSX, which he was known to give as gifts while the model was still in production. The car's suggested retail price was almost $90,000. Ellison also owns a private jet and is a licensed pilot, and he owns a yacht that he frequently enters in races.

Ellison was born August 17, 1944, in the Bronx to Florence Spellman. His mother was 19 years old and unwed at the time of his birth. At the age of nine months, after contracting pneumonia, he was adopted by his aunt and uncle, Lillian Spellman Ellison and Louis Ellison. He did not meet his biological mother again until he was 48.

He grew up in a middle-class Jewish neighborhood in Chicago. Though he and his adoptive father were distant, he had a very close relationship with his adoptive mother. When she died prior to Ellison's finals in his sophomore year at the University of Illinois at Urbana-Champaign, he dropped out. After spending the summer in Northern California, he enrolled at the University of Chicago for a semester but moved back California to pursue his interest in computer design.

While he was there, he worked for database companies. While working for Ampex, one of his primary projects was a database for the CIA, which he named "Oracle." In 1977 he founded a company that went through several name changes before finally settling on Oracle, after its flagship product, Oracle Database. The first version of Oracle released was called Oracle 2, to imply that all bugs had been worked out, though Oracle 1 had never been released. Since Oracle 2's release in 1979, Oracle has bought out 75 other technology-based companies—most recently, Sun Microsystems. Those 75 companies, combined with Oracle, are said to be worth over $40 billion.

Originally IBM held complete domination over the database market. Over the years, as IBM focused its efforts on large databases, it didn't enter the market for a Unix or Windows-based system until Oracle and a few other companies had found their niche there. As the early 1990s progressed, Oracle's competitors gradually went out of business, and it spent almost the entire decade at the head of the industry, with very little competition. In fact, Oracle had no major competition until the late 1990s when Microsoft's SQL Server began gaining popularity and IBM introduced software to complement its DB2 database.

Today IBM's DB2 still dominates the mainframe database market, but Oracle still holds a large portion of the markets based on UNIX, Linux, and Windows.

In 1997, Ellison was made a director of Apple Computers upon Steve Jobs' return to the company, though he resigned five years later, stating his inability to attend board meetings as the main cause of his resignation.

In 2009, Hewlett-Packard fired its CEO, Mark Hurd. Ellison called this the "worst personnel decision since the idiots on the Apple board fired Steve Jobs." A month later, Ellison's company hired Hurd as co-president, with Ellison remaining CEO. Around that same time, Ellison had his salary at Oracle reduced to $1. Despite this, he was named the highest-paid executive from 2000-2009, collecting $1.84 billion in salary and bonuses.

Ellison is currently the fifth wealthiest man in the world, according to Forbes, and his net worth is valued at $39.5 billion.

• Larry Page

Larry Page is the co-founder, along with Sergey Brin, and CEO of Google.

Page married Lucinda Southworth on Richard Branson's Necker Island in the Caribbean in 2007. Southworth is a research scientist who is the sister of actress and model Carrie Southworth. The Pages have one child.

Page was born on March 26, 1973, in East Lansing, Michigan. Both of his parents were computer science professors at Michigan State University. From an early age, Page was interested in computers. He loved taking things apart and decided he wanted to be an inventor. He earned a Bachelor of Science degree in computer engineering from the University of Michigan and a Masters Degree in computer science from Stanford University.

Page met Sergey Brin during new-student orientation at Stanford. They did not get along at all at first—in fact, each thought the other was obnoxious—but they eventually realized they had much in common and became close friends.

In the late 1990s, the two PhD candidates and Star Trek fans were contemplating what it would take to develop an all-knowing computer like the one on the Starship Enterprise. The duo decided to take on the challenge of improving the Internet search experience. Rather than sorting pages by analyzing words and their positions in the page, they based the relevance of each page by the number of links that connected to it. Page and Brin were not the first ones to come up with this solution, but they were the first to figure out the math and programming. Their iconic paper was titled "The Anatomy of a Large-Scale Hypertextual Web Search Engine."

They filled Page's room at Stanford with computers and tested an early prototype of Google. The pair soon moved their operation to a borrowed garage.

Page and Brin took leave from their PhD studies at Stanford while they worked to expand Google. Technically, they are still on leave.

At first, they were unsure how to market their search engine. They resisted ads at first, but eventually decided to sell them. Today Google earns over $2 billion per year from ads.

Google took off immediately, mostly due to its simple, user-friendly interface. Paid links are identified and there are no pop-up ads. Many users also enjoy the web site's whimsical artwork that changes on holidays and special occasions.

The company's motto of "Don't be evil," and its friendly company culture (which includes free food and encouragement for employees to spend 20% of their time working on personal projects) encourages the brightest to apply to work for it.

Today "to Google" has become a verb used worldwide, and Google has entered the realms of maps, news, and email with its Google Maps, Google Earth, Google News, and Gmail.

When China decided to censor the information that Google could provide, the company went along with the scheme at first. Eventually Google decided to take a stand and refused to go along any further, despite the potential of losing millions of dollars of revenue and attacks on Google allegedly by Chinese officials trying to hack into its database to locate government dissidents.

In 2004, Google.org was launched. The organization aims to solve worldwide problems concerning poverty, energy, and the environment. Projects include alternative and renewable energy such as an offshore wind farms, the Tesla electric car, and a car with artificial intelligence that can help drivers avoid accidents.

Page and Brin both were awarded honorary MBAs from IE Business School. They won the Marconi Foundation Prize for engineering and were elected Fellows of the Marconi Foundation at Columbia University as well as Fellows of the American Academy of Arts and Sciences. Page also received an honorary doctorate from the University of Michigan and was elected to the National Academy of Engineering.

As of 2011, Page's personal wealth is estimated to be $19.8 billion, tying him with Brin at 24th on the *Forbes* list of the richest people in the world.

Lee Shau-Kee

Lee Shau-Kee is a Hong-Kong-based real estate mogul. Because he is Chinese, his family name is Lee.

Lee is divorced, a rarity among Chinese businessmen. His ex-wife is Lau Wai-kuen. They have two sons, Peter and Martin, and a daughter, Margaret, as well as six grandchildren.

Lee was born on January 29, 1928, in Shunde, Guangdong, China, but soon moved to Hong Kong.

He is the founder, chairman of the board of directors, managing director, and majority owner of Henderson Land Development, a real estate conglomerate with interests in real property, hotels, restaurants and Internet services.

Lee is also the chairman of Hong Kong & China Gas Company, Limited, which is controlled by Henderson Land Development.

Lee's other positions include chairman of Henderson Cyber Limited; executive director of Henderson China Holdings Limited; vice chairman and independent non-executive director of Sun Hung Kai Properties, Limited; and chairman of the Miramar Hotel and Investment Company, Limited.

Additionally, he is a member of the boards of directors of Hong Kong Ferry (Holdings), Limited, and of the Bank of East Asia, Limited.

Lee has earned significant profits from his holdings of Mainland-China-controlled stocks such as PetroChina, China Shenhua Energy and China Life. One recent lucrative investment for the self-made billionaire was the initial public offering (IPO) for Nine Dragons, a paper company started by fellow Chinese billionaire Yan Cheung.

These hefty returns on investment have earned him several nicknames, including "Asia's Master of Stock" and "the Hong Kong Warren Buffett." He is also sometimes affectionately called "Uncle Four", because he is one of the few fourth-born children in China and the world to become a multi-billionaire.

In July 2010, police raided Henderson's offices as part of an investigation into canceled sales at a luxury apartment building owned by the developer; the company has denied the accusation of wrongdoing.

That same month, Lee's eldest son and heir to the vast empire became the father of triplet boys. The mother has not been identified, but there have been unconfirmed rumors that she was a surrogate living in the United States.

At the time the triplets were born, Lee's younger son Martin had two daughters. In 2011, Martin's wife gave birth to a son. Daughter Margaret has no children as yet.

It is important to Chinese magnates that they have male heirs, and triplets are especially desirable because the number three is a lucky number as it sounds like the Cantonese word for "birth." So Lee Shau-Kee decided to share his happiness and his wealth to celebrate the triplets' births by giving away 33 million Hong Kong dollars (about $4.3 million U.S.), of which HK$20 million was donated to Union Hospital in Hong Kong. The rest was divided among Henderson Land's approximately 1,300 employees; each received about HK$10,000.

Lee has advised investors to avoid United States currency and buy stock in Chinese companies. He is especially bullish on oil stocks.

Lee is a fan of soccer and belongs to a group that is trying to buy the Portsmouth, England, Football Club.

Lee is the chairman of Pei Hua Education Foundation Company, Limited, and honorary councilor of Rehabilitation International.

Lee's other philanthropic beneficiaries include the Chinese University of Hong Kong. In 1977, he became a member of what was then the University Advisory Board of the Three-Year MBA Programme and later renamed the Advisory Board of the MBA Programmes. He has also been a Member on the Board of Trustees of the United College since 1988.

Lee is also a major donor to the Chinese University, and, in 1993, the University awarded him an honorary doctor of social science degree. He has also donated to the CUHK-Yale South China Studies Programme, which has supported a collaboration between the University and Yale University.

In July 2007, the Hong Kong government awarded Lee the Grand Bauhinia Medal for public service.

As of 2011, *Forbes* estimates Lee to be worth $18.5 billion, ranking him the 2nd richest person in Hong Kong and the Greater China area and 28th richest in the world.

• Leonardo Del Vecchio

Leonardo Del Vecchio is the founder and chairman of luxury eyewear manufacturer Luxottica Group S.p.A.

Del Vecchio was born on May 22, 1935, in Milan, Italy, the fifth child of a widow. Del Vecchio's father died five months before he was born. When Leonardo was seven years old, his mother decided she could not afford to raise him and his four siblings by herself, so she gave him up to an orphanage.

Del Vecchio is married and has six children. His son, Claudio, recently sold his shares of failed U.S. fabric retailer Casual Corner but he still owns men's clothing retailer Brooks Brothers.

After graduating from high school, Del Vecchio began apprenticing to a tool and dye maker in Milan. He soon decided to put his metalworking skills to use making parts for eyeglasses. In 1961, he moved to the center of the Italian eyewear industry, the town of Agordo in the province of Belluno in the Veneto region. There he formed the limited partnership, Luxottica S.p.A. In 1967, Luxottica began selling eyeglass frames. The company now makes sunglasses and prescription frames under licenses from several renowned high fashion and trendy designers.

In 1974, Del Vecchio decided to acquire distribution company Scarrone.

Luxottica established a German subsidiary in 1981, the first of many international divisions.

In 1988, the company signed a licensing agreement with designer Armani. Other companies that Luxottica established deals with included Italian Vogue, Chanel, and Prada.

Luxottica soon acquired many additional eyewear chains such as LensCrafters, the U.S.-based international retailer of prescription eyewear and sunglasses. LensCrafters currently has 850 stores in the United States, Canada, Hong Kong, and Puerto Rico.

The company also purchased Australian company OPSM, the largest retailer of eyeglasses in Australia and New Zealand, which also has stores in Singapore, Malaysia, and Hong Kong.

The company also purchased Persol, the Italian eyewear company originally formed to make glasses for sportscar drivers and pilots. Persol is known for its sturdy sports sunglasses.

In 2007, Luxottica acquired Oakley, based in Foothill Ranch, California. Oakley is known not only for its prescription glasses, goggles, and sunglasses, but also for its luxury and designer sporting equipment that includes backpacks, shoes, clothing, and watches.

Luxottica also owns two Chinese retail eyeglass chains, Xueliang Optical and Ming Long Optical. Other brands owned by Luxottica include Ray-Ban, Sunglass Hut, Pearle Vision, Surfeyes, and Cole National. Luxottica is now the world's largest eyewear company.

Today Luxottica boasts over $3 billion in sales. The company's Sunglass Hut and Lenscrafters divisions include over 6,000 stores.

In addition to eyewear, Del Vecchio is the largest shareholder and Chairman of the Board of Directors of Italian real estate group Beni Stabili.

Over the years, Del Vecchio has acquired a reputation as a workaholic.

His 2011 net worth is estimated at $11 billion. He is the second-richest person in Italy and the 71st-richest in the world.

Li Ka Shing

Li Ka Shing, chairman of Hutchison Whampoa, Limited, and Cheung Kong Holdings, Limited, is an entrepreneur involved in many industries in Hong Kong and Canada, including telecommunications, shipping, and real estate. Li's business holdings are primarily in Hong Kong, but he is a Canadian citizen and splits his time between the two countries.

Li was born on June 13, 1928, in Chiu Chow on the southeast coast of China. His wife, Chong Yuet Ming, is deceased. He has two sons, Richard and Victor.

In 1940, Li and his family were forced to flee the mainland and moved to Hong Kong, where they stayed at the home of his rich uncle. Seeing his uncle's success made Li determined to make a success of his own life. Li later married the daughter of this uncle, his first cousin Chong Yuet Ming.

When Li was only 12 years old, his father died, leaving Li to take over responsibility for the family, so Li dropped out of school and went to work in a factory that manufactured plastic toys. It was a tough life for the young boy, with 16-hour workdays.

With money borrowed from family and friends, in 1950, Li started his own plastics manufacturing plant, specializing in making high-quality, low-cost plastic flowers. The company eventually grew to be the largest supplier of plastic flowers in Asia.

The Hong Kong Riots of 1967 caused many people to leave the island, and real estate prices crashed. When Li was unable to renew the lease on his plastics plant, he scooped up several parcels of this bargain basement priced land. To this day Li's strategy continues to be to buy up land when real estate prices become depressed.

Eventually Li's company, Cheung Kong, became Hong Kong's leading real estate investment entity. Li also holds personal stakes in real estate in Singapore and Canada, including sites in Vancouver and Toronto. Other Canadian holdings include Husky Energy, based in Alberta.

Cheung Kong also owns Hong Kong Electric Holdings Limited.

Additionally, Li is the owner of Cheung Kong Holdings, the world's largest health and beauty retailer, which went public on the Hong Kong Stock Exchange in 1972.

Li also acquired Hutchison Whampoa Limited (HWL), the world's largest operator of container ports. Hutchison Whampoa'e subsidiary, the A.S. Watson Group, is a leading retailer that consists of popular European brands such as Superdrug (UK), Marionnaud (France), and Kruidvat (Benelux countries), as well as Asian stores such as PARKnSHOP supermarkets, TASTE food gallerias, Fortress electrical appliances, Watson's Wine Cellars, Watson's Your Personal Store, and the Nuance-Watson duty free shops. ASW is also a major producer and distributor of water and beverages, with Watsons Water the best selling brand in Hong Kong. Hutchison Whampoa also owns almost 50% of Hutchison Telecommunications

High-tech holdings made through Li's investment company, Horizons Ventures, include shares in social networking site Facebook; music streaming service Spotify; and Siri, a virtual personal assistant iPhone app.

Li's philanthropic donations, including those through the charitable foundations named after himself in Hong Kong and Toronto, Canada, total over $1.41 billion so far. He has pledged to donate 1/3 of his massive fortune to charity, an amount that could reach $10 billion.

Philanthropic activities in higher education include establishing Shantou University near his hometown of Chaozhou, and donating $11.5 million to the Singapore Management University, $128 million to the University of Hong Kong Faculty of Medicine, $40 million to the University of California at Berkeley, $90 million to the Stanford University School of Medicine, and $100 million to the Lee Kuan Yew School of Public Policy at the National University of Singapore.

Additionally, Lee has donated over $33 million to earthquake relief efforts.

Li's many awards include the Knight Commander of the Order of the British Empire and the French Légion d'honneur.

The local media has given him the nickname of "Superman".

Li's son, Victor, is managing director and deputy chairman of Cheung Kong Holdings, while son Richard runs PCCW, a leading IT company and the largest telecom in Hong Kong. Both are citizens of Canada.

Although he owns a house in one of Hong Kong's most expensive neighborhoods, Deep Water Bay, Li has a reputation for leading a simple, frugal life, wearing an inexpensive watch, plain ties, and plain black shoes.

Li Ka Shing is the wealthiest man in Hong Kong and East Asia and the 11th richest in the world, with a net worth estimated at $26 billion.

• Liliane Bettencourt

Liliane Bettencourt is a businesswoman, socialite, and philanthropist.

She was born in France on October 21, 1922, the only child of L'Oréal cosmetics founder Eugène Schueller. She is married and has one daughter, Françoise, who was born on July 10, 1953.

Bettencourt owns several homes. Her primary residence is a luxurious mansion in the chic Paris suburb of Neuilly-sur-Seine. She also owns a posh home on the coast of Brittany that was built by her father in the 1920s, as well as an island in the Seychelles.

Bettencourt's mother died in 1927 when she was only five years old. After her mother's death, Liliane became extremely close to her father and even became jealous of the women in her father's circle. Her father never remarried.

When she was 15 years old, she became an apprentice in her father's company, mixing cosmetics and labeling shampoo bottles.

Just before World War II, Schueller began contributing money to a secret society called the CSAR (Comité Secret d'Action Révolutionnaire, or Secret Committee for Revolutionary Action), a fascist and anti-Communist organization. Schueller provided meeting space for the group at L'Oréal's Paris headquarters. This group was also known as La Cagoule (The Hood).

With the approval of the Germans, Schueller founded the Mouvement Social Révolutionnaire, or MSR (Revolutionary Social Movement) during the Nazi occupation of France. The group opposed Bolsheviks, capitalists, Jews, and Freemasons.

One of La Cagoule's members was André Bettencourt, who wrote pro-Nazi and anti-Semitic articles for La Terre Française (The French Land), a German propaganda paper. André has since recanted his Nazi sympathies, dismissing them as an "error of youth".

Toward the end of the war, after the allies invaded Normandy and it became obvious that the Nazi occupation was coming to an end, Schueller and André joined the Résistance. After the war, André managed to get collaboration charges against Schueller dismissed, citing his membership in the Résistance.

L'Oréal subsequently hired André and several other members of La Cagoule. André eventually became a government minister under Charles de Gaulle and served as deputy chairman of L'Oréal during the 1960s and 70s.

Liliane and André were married in 1950.

When her father died in 1957, Liliane inherited the L'Oréal business and became its principal shareholder. The company went public in 1963, but Bettencourt continues to own the majority of the stock. In 1974, Bettencourt traded about 50% of her L'Oréal stock for 3% of Nestlé S.A.

Liliane, Françoise, and Françoise's husband, Jean-Pierre Meyers, are all members of L'Oreal's Board of Directors.

Jean-Pierre is the grandson of a rabbi who was killed at Auschwitz. Françoise has converted from Catholicism to Judaism, and the couple is raising their two sons in the Jewish faith.

In 1987, Liliane, André, and Françoise founded La Fondation Bettencourt Schueller (The Bettencourt Schueller Foundation), located in Neuilly-sur-Seine. The foundation contributes mostly to medical and scientific, cultural and artistic, and humanitarian and social causes. One of its awards is the "Liliane Bettencourt Prize for Life Sciences," which is given to a top European biomedical researcher under the age of 45 each year.

Bettencourt's "golden years" have been plagued by scandal.

In 2004, L'Oréal was accused by Monica Waitzfelder of illegally usurping her Jewish family's home when it was seized by the Nazis during World War II.

In 2007, Liliane Bettencourt was caught funneling illegal campaign contributions to French president Nicolas Sarkozy through his employment minister, Eric Woerth.

She also had a scandal-ridden relationship with celebrity photographer François-Marie Banier, who has been labeled her gigolo by the French press. At one time she had disinherited her daughter, which is illegal under French law. However, she eventually booted Banier out and put her daughter Françoise back in the will. Françoise subsequently sued Banier for elder abuse for taking advantage of her mother by persuading her to sell with almost a billion Euros worth of art masterpieces, cash and life insurance.

Bettencourt's 2011 net worth is estimated at $16 billion. She ranks 15th in the world on *Forbes*' list of billionaires.

• Mark Zuckerberg

Mark Zuckerberg is co-founder, CEO, and president of social networking giant Facebook.

Zuckerberg lives in a $7 million house in Palo Alto, California, with long-time girlfriend Priscilla Chan. He has three sisters, Randi, Donna and Arielle, and is red-green colorblind.

Zuckerberg was born on May 14, 1984, in White Plains, New York, to Karen Zuckerberg, a psychiatrist, and Edward Zuckerberg, a dentist. The Zuckerbergs soon moved to Dobbs Ferry, New York. He and his sisters were raised in the Jewish faith, but he has since declared himself to be an atheist.

Zuckerberg was a computer-programming prodigy. When he was in elementary school, his father taught him BASIC programming and hired software developer David Newman to tutor him.

He attended Ardsley High School for two years. In his junior year, he transferred to Phillips Exeter Academy. Zuckerberg was a popular student and captain of the fencing team. He excelled in classical studies, science, and math.

Exeter's student directory, "The Photo Address Book," which was referred to as "The Facebook," later inspired the name of the social networking website.

Zuckerberg speaks and writes French, Hebrew, Latin, and ancient Greek, and often recites lines from classic epic poems such as Virgil's *Aenid* and Homer's *Iliad* and *Odyssey*. Additionally, he learned to speak Mandarin Chinese for a visit to Chan's relatives in Mainland China.

During high school, Zuckerberg took a graduate course in computer programming at Mercy College. He also developed a computer program that he dubbed "ZuckNet" that allowed his father's home-based dental office computer to communicate with the other computers in the house.

He built a media player, Synapse, that used artificial intelligence to learn users' listening habits. Microsoft and AOL tried to purchase Synapse and recruit Zuckerberg, but he declined.

In 2002 Zuckerberg entered Harvard, where he studied psychology and computer science and joined Alpha Epsilon Pi. It was at a fraternity party that he met Chan, a medical student from Braintree, Massachusetts.

Zuckerberg created a program called Facemash that let students choose the "hotter" person from two photos that he took from Harvard's "Face Books", which included the names and pictures of everyone who lived in the dormitories. The site was so popular that Harvard shut it down because the traffic overwhelmed its server. Additionally, some students protested that their photos were being used without permission. Zuckerberg issued a public apology, but when he heard that students were asking the university to develop an internal website that would include photos and contact information, he decided to develop one himself.

At first Facebook was confined to Harvard, but Zuckerberg and his roommate, Dustin Moskovitz, decided to expand it to other schools, including Dartmouth, Columbia, Cornell, Yale, and Stanford.

Shortly after Facebook launched in 2004, fellow Harvard student Wayne Chang announced i2hub, another campus-only service, that allowed peer-to-peer file sharing. In August of 2004, Zuckerberg and his friends Andrew McCollum, Adam D'Angelo, and Sean Parker launched a competing peer-to-peer file sharing service called Wirehog.

During the summer of 2004, after declining offers from several companies to buy Facebook, Zuckerberg, Moskovitz, and a few other friends moved to Palo Alto and met Peter Thiel, their first investor. The group had planned to return to Harvard but stayed in California.

In 2007, Zuckerberg announced Facebook Platform, a development platform that programmers could use to create applications for Facebook. Platform quickly grew to include over 800,000 developers around the world.

Facebook next initiated Beacon, which let Facebook users share information with their friends based on their activities on other sites. For example, eBay sellers could let their friends automatically know when they were selling something. Privacy advocates criticized the program as an invasion of privacy. Zuckerberg finally acknowledged these concerns and offered a way to opt out.

In 2008, Facebook Connect, a version of Facebook Platform for users, began operations. That same year Zuckerberg became the youngest billionaire in history.

Zuckerberg has repeatedly stated that he is more interested in enabling communication than making money through advertising. He calls himself a hacker and sponsors company-wide "hackathons" that he and other Facebook staff attend. The company provides food, beer, and music, and participants stay up all night trying to conceive and complete a project.

Zuckerberg and Facebook have been the target of several lawsuits.

Three Harvard students filed suit accusing Zuckerberg of leading them to believe he would help them build a social network called HarvardConnection.com, renamed ConnectU. The case was settled with Facebook agreeing to transfer more than 1.2 million shares and paying $20 million.

In 2007, court documents containing personal information about Zuckerberg and his family were posted on the website of *02138*, a magazine for Harvard alumni. Facebook filed to have the documents removed but the judge ruled in favor of the magazine.

Additionally a lawsuit filed by Eduardo Saverin claiming he was a co-founder of Facebook was settled out of court, with the company affirming Saverin's claim.

In 2010, Zuckerberg was voted *TIME* Magazine's Person of the Year.

Zuckerberg was portrayed by actor Jesse Eisenberg in the film, *The Social Network*, which was based on the book, *The Accidental Billionaires*. Both the book's author and the film's screenwriter admitted taking liberties with Zuckerberg's life and personality, making him appear to be socially incompetent and ruthless. Zuckerberg took the negative publicity with grace and a sense of humor, making a cameo appearance on Saturday Night Live when Eisenberg hosted.

The recipients of Zuckerberg's philanthropy include Diaspora, an open-source personal web server that implements a distributed social networking service, the Start-up: Education foundation, and the Newark Public

School system. Zuckerberg also signed the "Giving Pledge," whose signatories promise to donate at least 50% of their wealth to charity.

Zuckerberg's 2011 fortune is estimated by *Forbes* at $13.5 billion, placing him 52nd on the list of the world's billionaires.

Michael Bloomberg

Michael Bloomberg is the founder of financial data communications and media company, Innovative Market Systems, later renamed Bloomberg L.P. He is also the mayor of New York City.

He is divorced from first wife Susan Brown, with whom he has two daughters, Emma and Georgina. He lives with his girlfriend, Diana Taylor, a former New York state banking superintendent, on the Upper East Side of Manhattan.

Bloomberg was born in Boston, Massachusetts, on February 14, 1942. He is the grandson of Russian-Jewish immigrants. His father, William Henry Bloomberg, was a real estate agent. His mother, Charlotte Rubens Bloomberg, lived to the age of 102. His younger sister, Marjorie Tiven, is the Commissioner of the New York City Commission for the United Nations, Consular Corps and Protocol.

Bloomberg grew up in Allston, Brookline, and Medford, Massachusetts. He earned a Bachelor of Science degree in electrical engineering from Johns Hopkins University and an MBA from Harvard Business School.

In 1973, Bloomberg became a general partner at Salomon Brothers, first heading the equity trading division and then the systems development division. In 1981, after a merger, he was fired.

With the money from his $10 million golden parachute, Bloomberg established Innovative Market Systems, later renamed Bloomberg L.P. The company built and sold stock trading terminals called the Market Master. Merrill Lynch became the first customer to install the terminals and invested $30 million in the company. By 1987, the company had installed 5,000 terminals. The company now has over 250,000 terminals installed worldwide.

The company soon began marketing software services such as trading platform, Bloomberg Tradebook, and the Bloomberg Messaging Service. These subscription services send real-time financial data and research information directly to office terminals.

With the success of these services, the company expanded into television, radio, publishing, and the Internet. Bloomberg owns and operates a radio network that includes 1130 WBBR-AM in New York City; Bloomberg News is a major source of financial news.

Bloomberg gave up his position as CEO of Bloomberg L.P. in 2001 when he ran for the office of mayor of New York and was replaced as CEO by Lex Fenwick. The company president is now Daniel Doctoroff, Bloomberg's former deputy mayor.

A lifelong Democrat, Bloomberg abandoned his party to run for mayor after the September 11, 2001 attacks on the World Trade Center, succeeding termed-out Republican Rudy Giuliani. Bloomberg again switched allegiances and declared himself an Independent in 2007 but returned to the Republicans for his successful run at a third term in 2009.

Bloomberg has been the target of several sexual harassment and discrimination claims and lawsuits stemming from both his time at Bloomberg L.P. and his term as mayor.

He has also been accused of a participating in a conflict of interest when he campaigned for and signed the bill that would suspend New York's mayoral term-limit law to allow him to run for a third term.

He calls himself a fiscal conservative and a social liberal, supporting the pro-choice movement and gay marriage.

He has been awarded several honorary degrees, including a doctorate of public service from Tufts University, a doctorate of humane letters from Fordham University, a doctorate of laws from the University of Pennsylvania, and a doctorate of public service from George Washington University.

Bloomberg is well known for his philanthropy, having given away billions of dollars to charities. Among the recipients are Johns Hopkins University, the Sierra Club, the Campaign for Tobacco-Free Kids, the World Lung Foundation, the World Health Organization, and the Centers for Disease Control and Prevention. Bloomberg has also endowed the William Henry Bloomberg Professorship at Harvard in honor of his late father and the Temple Shalom, which was subsequently renamed the William and Charlotte Bloomberg Jewish Community Center, in honor of his parents. Along with Bill Gates, he has also pledged to help control tobacco use in developing countries. Additionally, he is reportedly an "anonymous" donor to the Carnegie Corporation, which supports causes such as the arts and individuals with cancer.

With a 2011 net worth estimated at $18.1 billion, Bloomberg is the 13th-richest person in the United States and tied for 30th on Forbes' list of the richest people in the world.

Michael Dell

Michael Saul Dell is best known as the founder and former CEO of one of the world's largest computer manufacturers, Dell Inc.

In 1988 he met his future wife, Susan Lieberman. Together, they have four children. He is largely viewed as an extremely shy and private individual, though recently he has become an extremely active user of the microblogging social network, Twitter.

He was born February 23, 1965, to a Jewish family residing in Houston, Texas. Dell's mother was a stockbroker and his father an orthodontist.

Dell showed signs of extreme business aspirations early on. At age 8 he applied to take a high school equivalency exam in order to jump-start his financial endeavors. When he was 12, he secured a job washing dishes at a local Chinese restaurant to finance a stamp and baseball card-trading venture. By his early teens, he had begun trading stocks and commodities purchased with earnings from various part-time jobs. At 15 he had purchased and immediately disassembled his first computer, an Apple II. One year in high school he was able to out-earn his economics teacher, amassing $18,000 by selling subscriptions to the Houston Post over the phone. His strategy: scanning mortgage and marriage applications to target new residents.

Unlike so many other computer industry moguls, Michael Dell did not begin his company in his parents' basement. Rather, it was his dorm room. While studying at University of Texas, Dell started a small business upgrading computers. He then began building computers, sold primarily to fellow Longhorns. His business model emphasized low prices, customer support, and product quality. He was able to achieve all of these profitably by selling products directly to customers, forgoing retail stores for product distribution. Innovations in the manipulation of distribution and supply chains would be a theme throughout Michael Dell's career. It is a huge factor in his success.

Dell soon began taking on bigger tasks like government contracts, which he obtained by underbidding other computer stores. By the end of his freshman year, his company was earning roughly $80,000 every month. This success made Dell's stay at the University of Texas brief. He dropped out after his freshman year.

In 1984, Dell registered his company under the name "PC's Limited." The business, now operating out of a small office, had sales totaling over $6 million in its first year alone—not bad, considering the company began as a $1,000 investment.

PC's Limited was incorporated under the new name Dell Computer Corporation in 1987. Shortly thereafter, it offered 3.5 million shares at $8.50 per share to the public. That year, Dell sales exceeded $150 million. Throughout the 1990s, Dell opened production centers throughout the world in order to expand its customer base to foreign markets. When the company began selling computers over the Internet, its daily sales quickly surpassed $1 million. By the end of 2002, sales would top $50 million per day.

As Dell Computers evolved and expanded, it maintained increasingly close relationships with its parts suppliers. It also utilized the Internet to integrate online orders with their suppliers, giving them access to up-to-date information about Dell orders, allowing Dell to purchase only what they needed, when they needed it. This strategy enabled Dell computers to drastically reduce its inventory without affecting operating efficiency.

In his book, *Direct from Dell: Strategies that Revolutionized an Industry*, Dell describes how he was able to keep Dell growing at such a high rate, discussing several mistakes he made and lessons he learned over the years. He also describes parts of his childhood.

In 2004, Dell temporarily stepped down as CEO of his company, though he remained involved in the company as its board chairman thereafter.

He has become somewhat of a philanthropist. In 1999, he and his wife created the Michael and Susan Foundation. The charity is mainly focused on causes related to children. Since its inception, the charity has provided over $500 million to various nonprofit organizations.

His investments are managed by MSD Capital L.P., an 80-employee company Dell founded for the sole purpose of handling his family's wealth. It has offices in Los Angeles, New York, and London, and deals mostly with securities, real estate and other private investments. Though its operations are not overseen by Michael Dell, and though it does not have any direct ties to Dell Inc., MSD Capital uses Dell computers exclusively.

Forbes estimates Dell's net worth to be around $13.5 billion as of March 2010. Before he briefly stepped down as CEO of Dell Computers, his net worth was close to $20 billion. He is the 44th richest man in the world.

Micky Arison

Micky Arison is the chairman of the board of directors and CEO of Carnival Corporation, the world's largest cruise ship operators.

Arison was born on June 29, 1949, in Tel Aviv, Israel, of Jewish descent. His father was Ted Arison, founder of Carnival. He has one sister, Shari.

Arison is married and has two children. The family's main residence is in Bal Harbour, Florida, and they also have homes in New York and Israel.

Arison briefly attended the University of Miami but dropped out in 1972 to go to work for his father's company in the sales department at Carnival, where he learned the business from the ground up.

In 1974, he became reservations manager and helped devise new marketing strategies for the cruise line. One of these strategies was a lower cost price plan that included shorter trips. Packages were all-inclusive, with airfare to and from the port, meals, and on-board activities and entertainment. This strategy helped Carnival to become competitive and attracted younger vacationers as well as older first-time cruisers.

In 1976, Arison became vice president of passenger traffic.

In 1978, Carnival announced that it was building the largest cruise ship in the world.

In 1979, Micky Arison took over from his father and became president of Carnival Corporation. Profits grew steadily and Arison oversaw the building of three additional ships. These ships were not typical cruise ships; rather they were their own self-contained vacation destinations with unique environments and amenities.

Under Arison's guidance, the company went public in 1987.

In 1990, his father stepped down as chairman of the board of directors and CEO, leaving Micky in charge of the company.

Arison continued to make acquisitions, including a stake in luxury line Seabourn Cruise Lines; Europe's leading cruise company, Costa Cruises; Holland America; and luxury operator Cunard Lines. These acquisitions helped Carnival enter the luxury cruise market and expanded its market share to about 50%.

Carnival was so successful that it operated at 100% capacity for several years, compared to the average 85% for its competitors.

At the turn of the 21st century, the economic recession began to affect Carnival's bottom line when vacationers became more frugal. The company cut its cruise prices by about 3%, the largest percentage of decline in nearly 20 years.

Arison also admitted that his company had erred when it consolidated the Seabourn and Cunard Lines in 1999, muddling the brands. Later that year, faulty engines caused a few of the cruise ships to go adrift, and several fires broke out. These problems caused potential cruisers to change their minds.

After the September 11th attacks, people cut back even more on their vacation plans, especially at locations they perceived as terrorist targets, including cruise ships. Added to all that, the insurance costs for cruise lines soared.

Arison and Carnival rebounded when they won a battle with Royal Caribbean to acquire 74% of P&O, the parent company of Princess Cruise Lines. The acquisition was a huge victory for Arison and Carnival, guaranteeing its position as the world's largest cruise company.

Arison has a reputation as an open-door, informal manager who believes in delegating work and allowing his employees to do their jobs without micromanagement.

Micky Arison also owns the Miami Heat basketball team. In 1995, when Arison became managing general partner of the Heat, he immediately hired Pat Riley, a head coach with proven success. The team soon became much more competitive, and in 2006 the Heat won the NBA championship. In 2010, they signed all-star players LeBron James and Chris Bosh and made it to the NBA finals, where they eventually lost to Mark Cuban's Dallas Mavericks. Arison also served as chairman of the NBA board of governors for three years.

Arison's 2011 net worth is estimated at $5.9 billion. He is currently ranked by *Forbes* as the 51st richest person in the United States and the 169th richest in the world.

Mukesh Ambani

Mukesh Ambani was born on April 19, 1957, in the Colony of Aden, which later became known as Yemen.

He is married to wife Nita. Along with their three children (Akash, Anant, and Isha), they live in a private two-story building in Mumbai, India, called Antilia. The house reportedly cost $1 billion to build, making it the most expensive in the world.

Mukesh Ambani is the oldest son of Dhirubhai Ambani, the late founder of Reliance Industries (RI), the largest privately owned business in India and one of the largest in the world. Mukesh has two sisters and one brother, Anil. Until the 1970s, Dhirubhai Ambani and his family lived in a two-bedroom apartment in Bhuleshwar, Mumbai.

Mukesh Ambani attended Abaay Morischa School in Mumbai and earned a bachelor's degree in chemical engineering from the University Department of Chemical Technology (UDCT) in Mumbai, India (formerly known as the University of Bombay). Mukesh later enrolled in the MBA program at Stanford University in California but was pulled out by his father to help with the business after one year.

When the Indira Gandhi administration allowed private parties to begin manufacturing PFY (polyester filament yarn) in 1980, Dhirubhai Ambani won the rights to set up a manufacturing plant. To help him build the PFY plant, he pulled Mukesh out of Stanford.

Mukesh initiated Reliance's transition from textiles to polyester fibers and later into petrochemicals, oil and gas exploration and production, and petroleum refining, creating one of the world's largest petroleum refineries in Jamngar, India. The petrochemicals plant can produce 20 million tons per year; the petroleum plant has an annual capacity of 660,000 barrels. RI's plans for the future include converting to a less polluting, low-carbon "green" natural gas.

Mukesh Ambani also created Reliance Infocomm Limited (now Reliance Communications Limited), one of the largest communications technology operations in the world.

Mukesh's brother, Anil, is also a billionaire and owns a competing company, Reliance Anil Dhirubhai Ambani Group. The two brothers have often clashed over business.

RI has been accused of receiving special favors from the government, which has allegedly allowed them to bend rules and violate the terms of their contract. RI has also been suspected of overinflating its natural gas and oil development costs, allowing it to sell its oil at three times the cost of government companies.

In July 2011, the Press Trust of India reported that a federal probe was being instigated against "leading private players and foreign consultants involved in oil and gas explorations." While the report did not name any of these companies, RI shares dropped 4% amid concerns that it might be one of those accused.

Mukesh Ambani owns 48% of RI and currently serves as Chairman of the Board of Directors and Managing Director.

Outside of RI, some of Ambani's many responsibilities include serving as a member of the board of directors of the Bank of America Corporation and the International Advisory Board of the Council on Foreign Relations. He also serves on the Prime Minister of India's Council on Trade and Industry, the World Economic Forum, and the United Nations Millennium Development Goals Advocacy Group. Ambani is Vice Chairman of the World Business Council for Sustainable Development and belongs to the International Advisory Boards of Citigroup and the National Board of Kuwait. Somewhat ironically, he also serves on the Advisory Council for the Graduate School of Business at Stanford University, the school from which he dropped out.

Ambani also owns the Indian Premier League soccer team, the Mumbai Indians.

In 2007, a combination of factors, including a major increase of the value of the Indian rupee, made him the richest man in the world. *Forbes* estimates that he will regain that position in 2014.

Ambani's 2011 wealth is estimated at $27 billion. He is the second richest man in Asia and the ninth richest in the world.

Patrick Soon-Shiong

Patrick Soon Shiong is the founder of cancer research firm American Bioscience, Incorporated (ABI) (later renamed Abraxis Bioscience), and its subsidiary, American Pharmaceutical Partners (APP).

He lives in Los Angeles, California, with his wife, actress Michele B. Chan, and their two children.

Soon-Shiong was born in South Africa in 1952, the son of a Chinese village doctor and herbal medicine practitioner who fled China during World War II. He graduated from the University of Witwatersrand Medical School. After finishing his internship at Johannesburg's General Hospital, he earned a Master of Science degree from the University of British Columbia.

In 1983 he moved to Los Angeles, where he began surgical training and teaching at UCLA Medical School. There he performed the school's first whole pancreas transplant. UCLA asked him to start their transplant program, but he wanted a less invasive way of curing diabetes. Rather than transplanting the entire organ, Soon-Shiong searched for a way to transplant only the islets, the cells that produce insulin. In prior islet transplants, patients' antibodies destroyed the cells before they could produce insulin, but Soon-Shiong developed a way to protect the islets by placing them inside capsules made of gel derived from seaweed. However, his results could not be validated and remain controversial.

Soon-Shiong left UCLA in 1984 and, with the help of older brother, Terrence, started a company named VivoRx to pursue a diabetes cure. Terrence claims he invested $2.5 million; Patrick says Terrence contributed nothing.

Soon-Shiong became obsessed with wrapping other drugs inside biologically active capsules to make them more powerful and significantly reduce side effects. He already had begun tinkering with cancer drugs, research that later would yield the breast cancer treatment drug Abraxane.

In 1993, the FDA approved human trials of the diabetes procedure. The first test was performed at St. Vincent's Medical Center in L.A. on a patient who had been suffering from diabetes and injecting insulin daily for over 30 years. The procedure worked, and the patient was eventually able to go for 30 days without an injection.

Rather than following the established protocol of publishing in a peer-reviewed journal, Soon-Shiong made the rounds of talk shows and conferences before publishing the results months later in the journal *Lancet*, earning him both celebrity status and the enmity of his colleagues.

In 1994, Milan Puskar of generic drug maker Mylan Laboratories agreed to invest $5 million in VivoRx for a 10% stake. He also agreed to fund the monthly research costs of $200,000.

Soon-Shiong then formed a second company, VivoRx Pharmaceuticals, which later was renamed American Bioscience, and then Abraxis Bioscience, to pursue research on a cancer drug named Abraxane. Puskar invested $1,000 for a 10% stake in the pharmaceutical company.

He worked on both diseases for four years but was more interested in the cancer research than the diabetes cure. In 1998, Puskar and brother Terrence fired Patrick and sued him for fraud, alleging that he had used consultants paid by VivoRx to work at American Bioscience and had redirected Mylan's money to cancer research. In early 1999, the case went to an arbitrator, who cleared Patrick of wrongdoing.

Terrence rehired Patrick but sued him again a year later. Patrick eventually agreed to pay $32 million to buy the rest of Mylan's ABI shares and fund diabetes research for three years. Patrick agreed to remain out of the diabetes field until June 2003, but he retained the patents to Abraxane. He remained at ABI and formed American Pharmaceutical Partners, taking it public but retaining a majority.

The diabetes research stalled. Terrence retains the patents but is doing little with them.

Meanwhile, ABI was criticized for making an unusual deal with APP, which it owned, that granted it exclusive North American manufacturing and sales rights to Abraxane for $60 million up front and another $25 million based upon achieving specified milestones.

In 2008, Soon-Shiong sold his stake in APP to Fresenius SE for $3.7 billion and sold ABI to Celgene for $2.9 billion in 2010.

Soon-Shiong serves on the board of advisors of RAND Health and the boards of the Mendez National Institute of Transplantation and Northwestern University's Technology Council for the Center for Cancer Nanotechnology Excellence. He is the executive director of the UCLA Wireless Health Institute and chairman of the National Coalition for Health Integration.

Soon-Shiong has angered his neighbors by secretly buying up multiple properties in a middle-class neighborhood of Brentwood, California, to construct a McMansion that is expected to take up 18,000 square feet on three acres.

Soon-Shiong became part owner of the Los Angeles Lakers basketball team when he bought the shares of Earvin "Magic" Johnson in 2010.

He is a Fellow of the Royal College of Surgeons (Canada) and a Fellow of the American College of Surgeons.

Soon-Shiong has donated to St. John's Health Center in Santa Monica and made a $100-million pledge to reopen Martin Luther King, Jr., Hospital in Los Angeles. He has signed the Warren Buffett/Bill and Melinda Gates pledge to give away half his fortune to charity.

In 2011, *Forbes* estimated his worth at $5.2 billion, ranking him at #195.

• Phil Knight

Phil Knight is the co-founder and chairman of the board of directors of Nike, Inc. He lives in Oregon with his wife, Penny. They have two sons and a foster daughter.

He was born in Portland, Oregon, on February 24, 1938, the son of a loving but tough father, William H. Knight (the publisher of the now-defunct *Oregon Journal*) and a homemaker, Lola.

Too small to play contact sports, Knight began running track at an early age. When Knight's father refused to give him a summer job at his paper, Knight got a job at its rival, *The Oregonian*, working the night shift tabulating sports scores. Every morning he ran seven miles home.

While Knight was attending the University of Oregon, he ran middle-distance track for legendary coach Bill Bowerman. Knight graduated in 1959 with a degree in journalism and went on to study at the Stanford Graduate School of Business.

While at Stanford, Knight realized that he wanted to be an entrepreneur. He wrote a paper, "Can Japanese Sports Shoes Do to German Sports Shoes What Japanese Cameras Did to German Cameras?" that served as a blueprint for his business plan to develop a low-cost, high-quality running shoe.

After receiving his master's degree in business administration from Stanford in 1962, Knight took a trip around the world, stopping in Kobe, Japan, in November 1962. There he found Tiger brand running shoes. Knight met with the manufacturer, Mr. Onitsuka, and obtained the distribution rights for the western U.S.

Upon returning to Portland, Knight took a job as an accountant while he waited for the shoe samples. When they arrived, Knight sent two pairs to Bill Bowerman, hoping to gain an endorsement. Bowerman not only ordered the shoes, he also offered to partner with Knight in the new venture and to provide some new designs for better shoes. The two formed Blue Ribbon Sports, the predecessor of Nike, on January 25, 1964.

Knight started selling shoes out of his car, a Plymouth Valiant, at track meets in the Pacific Northwest. The company soon changed its name to Nike. Sales went well and Knight quit his accounting job to work full-time at the shoe venture. The company also got endorsements from legendary runners such as Steve Prefontaine and Alberto Salazar.

By the mid-1970s, Nike was at the forefront of sports shoe technology. Bowerman invented the famous waffle sole design when he poured liquid latex into his wife's waffle iron. The latex soles were springy and comfortable.

At a time when large manufacturers such as Adidas and Puma were manufacturing in European countries with high wages, Nike forged relationships with companies in the Far East, where developing countries were just beginning to establish manufacturing plants and wages were substantially lower.

The company got another endorsement break in the 1980s when tennis star Jimmy Connors won Wimbledon wearing a pair of Nikes and John McEnroe started wearing them after he hurt his ankle. Annual sales of the model worn by McEnroe shot up from 10,000 to over 1.2 million, and Nike was suddenly worth $178 million.

One area in which Nike stumbled was aerobics shoes. The "old boys" who made up the Nike board of directors failed to see the market for lightweight shoes for women to wear to their exercise classes, which they scoffed at as "fat ladies dancing." That mistake cost them dearly when Reebok cornered the market. The company belatedly realized the error of its ways, but, to this day, Nike and Reebok compete for dominance in aerobics footwear.

The company expanded its product lines to include clothing, accessories, and sporting equipment for men, women, and children.

Nike's Oregon campus is known for its employee perks such as its three restaurants, beauty salon, fitness center, laundry service, and day-care center.

But not all Nike workers have access to those amenities. In 1996, author and filmmaker Michael Moore, in his book *Downsize This!,* shed light on the harsh working conditions at Nike's Indonesian factories, sweatshops in which girls as young as fourteen and pregnant women labored. To his credit, of the almost 20 CEOs whom Moore wanted to interview, Knight was the only one who agreed. The interview is featured in Moore's film, *The Big One*.

While Knight pointed out that Indonesia was in the process of moving from farm labor to semiskilled industrial work and that Nike was providing them with hope for their future, in 1998, Nike imposed rules for better working conditions and began monitoring its contractors for compliance to the new rules.

Nike has also been criticized for the high prices of many of its popular shoes, especially those endorsed by basketball star Michael Jordan. Some maintain that the price of over $100 is too much for Nike's target market of poor, inner-city youth to afford.

In 2002, Knight bought Will Vinton Studios, where his son, Travis, worked as an animator, and changed its name to LAIKA. Travis was elected to the board of directors and became CEO of LAIKA in 2009. LAIKA released its first feature film, *Coraline,* in 2009.

In November of 2004, Knight resigned as Nike's CEO but remained as chairman.

Knight was inducted into the Oregon Sports Hall of Fame for his Special Contribution to Sports in Oregon.

Phil and Penny Knight's philanthropy includes donations to the University of Oregon, the University of Oregon Athletics Legacy Fund, the Stanford Graduate School of Business, and his alma mater, Cleveland High School, for a new track, football field, and gymnasium. The Knights also pledged $100 million to the OHSU Cancer Institute, which was renamed the OHSU Knight Cancer Institute.

As of 2011, Knight's estimated net worth is $12.7 billion, making him the 60th richest person in the world.

Ralph Lauren

Ralph Lauren is an American designer who co-founded Polo Fashions.

He is married and the father of three sons, Andrew, David and Dylan. He lives primarily in Manhattan, New York, but also owns homes in Bedford and Long Island, New York, one on the island of Jamaica, and a ranch in Colorado.

Lauren was born Ralph Lifshitz on October 14, 1939, the youngest of four boys in a family of Russian-Jewish descent in the Bronx, New York. His father was an artist who supported the family by painting houses; his mother was a homemaker. Tired of being teased by their high-school classmates, he and his older brother eventually changed their last name to Lauren.

From an early age, Ralph bought expensive suits with money he earned at an after-school job.

After high school, Lauren moved to New York City, where he studied business at Baruch College at the City College of New York at night while working two part-time jobs as a glove salesman at Brooks Brothers during the day. He dropped out of school before receiving his degree.

Lauren served in the United States Army from 1962-1964. After his discharge, on December 20, 1964, Lauren married Ricky Anne Low-Beer, whom he had met in the eye doctor's office where she worked as a receptionist.

Lauren then went to work for tie manufacturer A. Rivetz & Co. While working at Rivetz he began to design a line of wide ties.

In 1968, with his tie designs and a $50,000 loan from Norman Hilton, Lauren and his brother Terry co-founded Polo Fashions, whose name they chose because of the lifestyle associated with the sport.

In the late 60s, Lauren approached Bloomingdale's to get them to sell his ties, but they wanted Lauren to make the ties narrower and remove his name from the label. Lauren refused to give in to the demands. Bloomingdale's eventually came back and begged Lauren to allow them to sell his fashions.

Lauren released his iconic Polo knit shirt in 1972. The shirt with its embroidered polo player went on to become the symbol of generations of preppies.

Lauren's next big break came in 1974 when the male actors in "The Great Gatsby" wore clothes from his fashion line, which fit in perfectly with the lost era of elegance evoked in the film. Lauren next created the costumes for Woody Allen's 1977 film, "Annie Hall". Allen's clothing consisted of traditional tweeds, button-down shirts, and chinos, while female star Diane Keaton wore a quirky blend of pieces from Lauren's lines for both men and women.

At the beginning of the 1980s Polo was considered the "power" suit. Lauren's clothing styles suited businessmen who wanted to look powerful yet stylish. In 1983 Lauren released a home collection of linens, furniture, and accessories. He later released a line of jeans as well as a line of children's clothing and accessories.

A few years later, after Georgio Armani's Italian look took over in popularity, Lauren fought back and reclaimed his position with a line of sophisticated American menswear.

Lauren was the first fashion designer to have his own store. Today the company operates approximately 275 retail stores in the United States and licenses over 100 worldwide.

Lauren still owns about 90% of Polo's shares.

In April 1987, Lauren underwent successful surgery to remove a benign brain tumor; he has since made a full recovery.

An avid collector of antique and sports cars, Lauren owns a collection that includes a 1929 Blower Bentley, a 1930 Mercedes-Benz CountTrossi SSK, a 1938 Alfa Romeo 8C 2900B Mille Miglia, a Bugatti Type 57SC Atlantic, a Porsche 997 GT3 RS, and two Ferrari 250 Testa Rossas.

Lauren has received many awards, including the Council of Fashion Designers of America (CFDA) Womenswear Designer of the Year for 1995, its Menswear Designer of the Year for 1996, and its Lifetime Achievement Award, as well as the French government's Chevalier de la Légion d'Honneur.

Lauren's philanthropic activities include the Ralph Lauren Center for Cancer Care and Prevention.

As of 2011, Forbes estimates Lauren's net worth at $5.8 billion, making him the 173rd richest person in the world.

Richard Branson

Sir Richard Branson is the founder and chairman of Virgin Group.

He lives in London with his second wife, Lady Joan Templeman. He is the father of one son and two daughters, one of whom died when she was only four days old. Branson also owns a private island in the Caribbean, Necker Island.

Branson was born on July 18, 1950, in Blackheath, London, England. His parents were Edward, a barrister, and Eve, a former dancer, actress, and flight attendant. He had a rough time in academics during school due to his dyslexia but excelled in sports, especially swimming.

At the age of 16, Branson dropped out of school, moved to London, and launched a highly successful music magazine named *Student*. He ran ads for records in the magazine and started a discount record mail order store, which eventually became Virgin Megastores. He and his partners chose the name because they were new at business.

Virgin sold records at much lower prices than regular record stores. Some of the records he sold were supposed to be for export only; eventually Branson settled out of court, agreeing to pay a fine along with unpaid taxes.

Branson's next venture was recording label Virgin Records. The label's first big hit was Mike Oldfield's *Tubular Bells*, whose sales skyrocketed after it was used on the soundtrack of *The Exorcist*. Virgin soon gained a reputation for signing avant-garde artists such as The Sex Pistols and Culture Club.

In 1984, Branson entered the transportation business with Virgin Atlantic Airways, which eventually grew to include subsidiaries such as Virgin Blue, Virgin Express, Virgin Nigeria, and Virgin America.

In the early 1990s after the global recession hit, Branson was forced to sell Virgin Records to EMI for £500 million to keep the airlines afloat. Branson later re-entered the music industry with V2 Records.

The company added Virgin Trains to its holdings in 1993; in 1999 it entered the telecommunications business with Virgin Mobile, which Branson later sold for nearly £1 billion, plus an annual license fee of £8.5 million.

In 2004, Branson announced plans to enter the space tourism industry with Virgin Galactic. The company licenses technology from Microsoft co-founder Paul Allen's Spaceship One, designed by legendary aeronautical engineer Burt Rutan.

Other Virgin products and ventures include cola, vodka, healthcare, animation, and comics.

Branson's private holdings are in a convoluted web of trusts and holding companies ranging from England to the British Virgin Islands.

After a breakfast meeting with Al Gore, Branson became interested in efforts to alleviate global warming. Branson founded Virgin Fuels attempting to develop a cheap, greener fuel for automobiles and aircraft. He also established The Virgin Earth Challenge, an award of $25 million for the first product to remove greenhouse gasses from the atmosphere every year for ten years.

Along with Nelson Mandela and musician Peter Gabriel, Branson formed a think-tank called The Elders to solve humanity's problems. Other members of the group include Archbishop Desmond Tutu, U.N. leader Kofi Annan, and former President Jimmy Carter.

Other philanthropy includes the Branson School of Entrepreneurship, the Sekenani Primary School in Kenya, the Global Zero campaign to eliminate nuclear weapons, the International Rescue Corps, Prisoners Abroad, and numerous green initiatives.

Branson was knighted by Queen Elizabeth II in 1999 for services to entrepreneurship. Other honors include the Tony Jannus Award for accomplishment in commercial air transportation, the U.N. Correspondents Association Citizen of the World Award, and an honorary doctorate from Loughborough University.

Branson was the first person to cross the Atlantic Ocean in a hot-air balloon; the balloon, the Virgin Atlantic Flyer, was the largest ever flown. He also holds the record for the fastest crossing in the Virgin Atlantic Challenger II. Other records include the fastest crossing of the Pacific Ocean and the fastest crossing of the English Channel in an amphibious vehicle. Several attempts at circumnavigation with adventurer Steve Fossett were unsuccessful.

Branson also owns Virgin Racing and is involved in research to develop cleaner fuels.

He is an avid skier and speedboat racer.

Branson has been parodied and played himself on many television shows and movies including *The Simpsons, Superman Returns,* and *Around the World in 80 Days.*

In August 2011, Branson's Necker Island home was destroyed by a lightning fire. Although Branson lost hundreds of photographs and papers, all of the guests managed to escape without injury, including Branson's 90-year-old mother, who was helped to safety by Oscar-winning actress Kate Winslet.

Forbes estimates Branson's 2011 fortune at $4.2 billion, making him the fifth richest person in the United Kingdom and 254th in the world.

Robin Li

Robin Li is the co-founder, Chairman of the Board of Directors, and Chief Executive Officer (CEO) of Baidu, the Chinese search engine giant.

His birth name is Li Yanhong, which he Americanized to Robin Li.

Li lives in Beijing, China, with his wife, Dongmin (Melissa) Ma (who also owns a share of Baidu), and their daughter. Li was born on November 17, 1968, in Yangquan in the Shanxi Province of Northern China, the fourth of five children and the only son of factory workers who pushed him to work hard so he could get into college.

While in high school, Li showed an affinity for computers and participated in numerous citywide programming competitions. He studied library information management at Peking University. During his studies, the university was closed for a year after the anti-government, pro-democracy riots in Tiananmen Square. Despite the interruption in his studies, Li graduated with a Bachelor of Arts and Science in information management in 1991. Li was accepted into the masters' program at the State University of New York at Buffalo. He graduated from SUNY with an MS in computer science in 1994.

Li began his career at IDD Information Services, a New Jersey division of Dow Jones and Company, where he helped to develop a software program for the Wall Street Journal's online edition.

While at IDD, Li became interested in search engines and developed the RankDex site-scoring algorithm, which is very similar to that of Google, ranking web sites based on how many other sites link to them. Li received a U.S. patent for this technology, which was later used as the basis for Baidu.

In 1997, Li moved to Northern California and joined Infoseek, one of the pioneers in the Internet search engine industry, as head of search engine development. Li stayed at Infoseek for two years but left when the company began to focus more on content.

In 2000, he and his friend, biochemist Eric Xu (Xu Yong) moved back to China and co-founded Baidu. The company's name translates to "One hundred times" and refers to a Song Dynasty poem regarding tenaciously searching for the sublime.

The pair set up shop in a hotel room across from Peking University. Li became chairman, while Xu became CEO.

Baidu was an immediate success with China's estimated 457 million—and growing—Internet users, eventually claiming 60%-70% of the market.

When the company restructured in 2004 and Xu's duties were substantially reduced, he resigned and returned to the biotechnology field. Li took over as CEO, and the company went public on the NASDAQ in 2005.

But with success came controversy and accusations of illegal and underhanded activity. Baidu has been sued by several music companies alleging copyright violations for Baidu's links to downloadable music. The company has also been accused of inflating its hit counts. Google and some media have complained that Baidu acquiesces to and even assists the Chinese government in censoring access to and content on the Internet.

In 2008, China Central Television reported that Baidu was including mostly paid advertisers in its search results while excluding companies that did not pay, and that some of these paid links were to pharmaceutical companies that were unlicensed. A few days after the CCTV report, Li and Baidu issued a public apology in a conference call. Li denied excluding non-paying companies but said it had cancelled the paid search listings for unlicensed firms. But the damage was already done and the company's stock price dropped by nearly a third.

Shares have since recovered. In 2010, Google threatened to pull out of the Chinese market in an ongoing battle with the Chinese government over censorship issues, sending Baidu usage and shares skyrocketing.

Future plans for Li and Baidu include a move into online video and expansion into international markets.

Li is also a member of the board of directors of New Oriental Education & Technology Group, Inc., an educational services provider in China.

Li is the author of the 1998 book, *Business War in Silicon Valley*.

With a fortune estimated at $9.4 billion, Li is the richest man in mainland China and is listed at 94th on the *Forbes* 2011 list of the world's wealthiest people.

• Ron Burkle

Ron Burkle is a U.S. businessman. He was born on November 12, 1952, in Pomona, California.

Burkle's father owned a grocery store where Burkle worked as bag boy as a teenager. He later worked at a Stater Bros. grocery store doing the same job. After Burkle dropped out of Cal Poly Pomona, he returned to Stater Bros. where he eventually worked his way into management. He was later fired from Stater Bros. when he attempted to buy the chain.

When he was 21 and she was 19, Burkle married Janet Steeper, a descendent of one of the Wright brothers. They are divorced and have three children and one grandchild.

Thanks in part to profits from trading Michael Milliken's junk bonds, Burkle formed The Yucaipa Companies, a private equity firm, and began buying and selling properties, especially grocery stores and chains. Since 1986, Yucaipa has reportedly completed mergers and acquisitions that total more than $30 billion.

Burkle has served on the boards of directors of many companies, including Wild Oats Markets, which were later sold to Whole Foods; Dominick's; Golden State Foods, one of McDonald's largest suppliers; Ralphs and Food4Less Markets, which he sold to Kroger; Occidental Petroleum Corporation; KB Homes; and Yahoo!

Burkle is co-owner of the Pittsburgh Penguins hockey team, along with hockey great Mario Lemieux. His cash infusion helped return the team to profitability and competitiveness, and the team won the Stanley Cup in 2006. Burkle and the Penguins recently built a new hockey stadium. Burkle also allegedly made a hostile takeover offer to buy the Pittsburgh Pirates baseball team. The offer was summarily rejected.

Burkle owns slightly less than 20% of booksellers Barnes and Noble, just under the target that would trigger the poison pill that B&N adopted specifically to repel his attempted takeover from family members who own 39% of the company.

Burkle is well-known for secretly videotaping two meetings between himself and ex-New York Post gossip columnist Jared Paul Stern with the help of his lawyers, the U.S. attorney's office, and the FBI. During the meetings, Stern attempted to extort a $220,000 investment in his clothing business in exchange for favorable Page Six coverage. The Post later fired Stern.

Burkle has also hired the mother of friend Reverend Jesse Jackson's illegitimate child and persuaded one of the heirs to the Anheuser Busch fortune to give Jackson's son, Yusef, a job at the company.

Burkle has contributed tens of millions of dollars both to Democrats in California, including State Senator Dianne Feinstein, and those in the rest of the United States. He contributed to Hilary Clinton's race for President.

Burkle tried to use his clout with the Democrats to get Bill Clinton to pardon Milliken, but he was unsuccessful. After Bill Clinton left the presidency, Burkle employed him at Yucaipa to the tune of $15 million, purportedly to locate possible targets in low-income areas for Burkle to acquire and develop.

Burkle has been embroiled in the midst of a nasty divorce from the mother of his three children for several years. His ex-wife has filed a request for an order of protection from him and accused him of invading her privacy by hiring detectives to follow her. She has also accused him of hiding his assets. In return, he accused her of attempting to kidnap his children and of endangering them by having an affair with her personal trainer, who has a criminal record. A law that was allegedly intended to specifically benefit Burkle that allowed divorce records to be sealed, allegedly to protect his "business interests" from becoming public, was passed by the Democratic-controlled California legislature and signed by ex-California governor Arnold Schwarzenegger, to whom Burkle had given a $200,000 campaign contribution. The courts later deemed that law to be unconstitutional, but a similar law was subsequently passed.

Burkle's Beverly Hills mansion was built by silent film legend Harold Lloyd. The house is reportedly worth over $30 million. Burkle has also owned several aircraft, including Sikorsky helicopter and a Boeing 757 jetliner.

As of 2011, Burkle's fortune is worth $3.2 billion. He ranks #110 in the United States and #347 in the world.

• Rupert Murdoch

Keith Rupert Murdoch is the chairman and CEO of News Corporation, a media conglomerate.

Murdoch is a naturalized American citizen who was born on March 11, 1931, in Melbourne, Australia. Twice divorced, he lives in New York with current wife, Wendi Deng, vice-president of STAR TV. Murdoch has two children with her: Grace, and Chloe. He has four other children as well: Prudence, Elisabeth, Lachlan, and James.

Murdoch's father, Keith, was a war correspondent and newspaper magnate. His mother, Elisabeth, was a life governor of the Royal Women's Hospital in Melbourne and established the Murdoch Children's Research Institute.

Murdoch was co-editor of his school paper and editor of the student journal. He worked part time at the *Melbourne Herald* and was groomed at an early age to take over the family business.

Murdoch studied philosophy, politics, and economics at Oxford University. After Oxford, Murdoch became a reporter for the *Birmingham Gazette* and an apprentice at the *London Daily Express*, learning from Lord Beaverbrook how to build circulation.

When his father died, Murdoch returned to Australia at age 21 to take over the family business, News Limited. He revived the failing *Adelaide News* and went on to buy and revive several more, including *The Perth Sunday Times, The Daily Mirror,* and *The Sydney Daily and Sunday Paper,* turning most of them into racy tabloids.

In 1964 he bought a controlling interest in New Zealand's daily paper, *The Dominion*. Later the same year he launched a serious daily Australian national paper, *The Australian*.

He expanded his empire into the U.K in 1969, taking over *The News of the World*, then the world's largest-circulation English-language paper. He also acquired *The Sun*, building it into a best-seller with the same gossip-and-scandal formula he applied in Australia. *The Sun* became his most profitable paper.

In 1972, Murdoch acquired the Sydney morning tabloid *The Daily Telegraph.*

He moved to New York in 1974 and expanded into the US market, acquiring *The San Antonio Express and News* and starting the weekly tabloid *The National Star.*

In 1976 Murdoch bought highly regarded liberal paper, *The New York Post*, transforming its image and doubling circulation. Murdoch then acquired *New York* magazine, *The Village Voice, The Boston Herald*, and *The Chicago Sun-Times.*

In 1981 Murdoch bought the failing but prestigious *London Times*.

Because only US citizens are legally permitted to own US television stations, Murdoch became naturalized in 1985. He expanded into the media and entertainment fields when News Corporation acquired Twentieth Century Fox. The movie studio produced blockbusters, *Titanic* and *Avatar*, while the network produced TV hits such as *The Simpsons* and *House*. News Corporation now owns television stations and networks around the world.

In 1986, Murdoch consolidated his UK printing operations and introduced electronic production. The resulting layoffs of 6,000 workers angered print unions, instigating a bitter and violent dispute. In 1987, the workers accepted a settlement of £60 million.

During the 1980s and early 1990s, Murdoch supported British Prime Ministers Margaret Thatcher and John Major, but he later supported Tony Blair and his Labour Party, holding secret meetings to discuss national policies. Murdoch and former Prime Minister Gordon Brown reportedly held regular communications. Murdoch eventually switched back to the Conservative Party, endorsing David Cameron. In 2008, Cameron accepted free flights on a private Gulfstream IV belonging to Murdoch's son-in-law, Matthew Freud. The flights were valued at £30,000. Murdoch and Cameron held private talks and attended private parties aboard Murdoch's yacht, the *Rosehearty*.

During the 1990s Murdoch entered the Asian and South American markets by snatching up local and national television stations.

In 1999, Murdoch expanded his music holdings in Australia by acquiring a controlling share in Australian label, Mushroom Records, later merged with Festival Records, forming Festival Mushroom Records (FMR).

By 2000, News Corporation owned more than 800 companies in at least 50 countries with a net worth totaling over $5 billion.

In 2003, Murdoch acquired a stake in Hughes Electronics, operator of DirecTV; in 2007, he bought Dow Jones, giving him control of *The Wall Street Journal* and *Barron's*.

While Murdoch was building his global empire, he delved into politics, spreading his influence among political parties and candidates. He hosted a fund-raiser for Senator Hillary Clinton and endorsed Barack Obama's presidential campaign, while at the same time donating millions to the Republican Governors Association and serving on the board of Libertarian Cato Institute.

In 2011, the UK and US governments launched investigations into charges that *The News of the World* had repeatedly and illegally hacked into telephones of government officials and private citizens, including the cell phone of a murdered teenage girl, hampering the investigation into her death. Former CEO Rebekah Brooks was allowed to resign in disgrace. Les Hinton, head of *The Wall Street Journal* at the time of the illegal activities, also resigned. Brooks and Rupert and James Murdoch were called to testify before Parliament. Rupert claimed he was not responsible for the actions of his subordinates and was completely unaware of the hacking, but letters later surfaced seemingly showing that all three not only knew about the hacking but also encouraged it. In mid-July, News International published letters signed by Murdoch apologizing for the "serious wrongdoing" and giving details about steps the company was planning to address the issue.

Murdoch also faces police and government investigations into bribery and corruption in the UK as well as FBI investigations in the US.

Murdoch's 2011 wealth is estimated at $7.6 billion, placing him at 117th on *Forbes'* list of the richest people on Earth.

Samuel Newhouse

Samuel Newhouse, Jr., is chairman of the board of directors and chief executive officer (CEO) of Advance Publications, the nation's largest privately owned newspaper chain.

Newhouse, who goes by the nickname of Si, lives in New York City, New York, with his wife. They have three children. He is the son of Samuel Newhouse, Sr., himself the son of a Russian-Jewish immigrant, who turned the *Bayonne Times* into Advance Publications. He was born in New York City on November 8, 1927. Newhouse grew up in New York and graduated from the city's public Horace Mann High School.

When the senior Newhouse died in 1979, Si and his brother, Donald, took over Advance, after winning a prolonged battle with the IRS over inheritance taxes.

Today, Si is in charge of the company's Condé Nast division, which publishes magazines such as *Vogue, Men's Vogue, Teen Vogue, Vanity Fair*, and *Glamour* magazines; and Fairchild, publisher of *Details, Women's Wear Daily*, and *W*. Don heads the newspaper operations, which publishes papers such as *The Staten Island Advance, The Cleveland Plain Dealer, The Birmingham News, The Times-Picayune*, and *The Newark Star-Ledger*.

Other iconic titles published by the Newhouse brothers include *Architectural Digest, The New Yorker, Bride, Bon Appétit, GQ*, and *House and Garden*.

The magazine division has entered full-bore into the men's arena with titles such as shopping magazine *Cargo, Golf Digest*, and *The Sporting News*.

In 2007, the brothers launched a business magazine headed by former *Wall Street Journal* editor, Joanne Lipman.

The Newhouse brothers' property with the largest circulation is *Parade* magazine, which is delivered every Sunday in newspapers throughout the United States.

Si Newhouse has been known to personally hand count the advertising pages in Condé magazines and those of its competitors.

The brothers have expanded the company and diversified into cable television and currently own Bright House Cable, with well over 2 million subscribers, as well as large stakes in Discovery Communications, which operates The Learning Channel, and Animal Planet.

They also have holdings in television news with their Bright House Networks, which operates entities such as Central Florida News 13 and the Bright House Sports Network.

The company also owns CondéNet, the Internet operator of web sites such as foodie site Epicurious and travel site Concierge. An affiliated company, Advance.net, has many (possibly all) of the Advance Publications print titles on line, as well, including publications ranging from lehighvalleylive.com (covering the Lehigh Valley) to NJ.com (covering New Jersey).

Samuel Newhouse and his wife are well-known for their generous philanthropic endeavors, including a $15 million donation they made to Syracuse University.

Newhouse is also a notable art collector and has owned works by Rubens, one of the Dutch Masters. He also owns one of the most valuable paintings in the world, a Jackson Pollock "drip" painting entitled No. 5, 1948. Newhouse was listed by *Art News* as one of the top 200 art collectors in the world.

Si's grandson, S. I. Newhouse IV, was featured in the documentary film *Born Rich*.

Samuel Newhouse's 2011 net worth is estimated at $6.6 billion. He is tied for 149th on *Forbes* list of the richest people in the world.

• Sergey Brin

Sergey Brin is one of the co-founders of Google, along with Larry Page. Brin lives in San Francisco with his wife, Anne, and their child.

He was born on August 21, 1973 in what was then the Soviet Union. Brin's father, Michael, is a mathematics professor at the University of Maryland. His mother, Eugenia, is a researcher at NASA's Goddard Space Center.

Michael and Eugenia are Russian Jews who felt the harsh reality of anti-Semitism in their early careers. Both were graduates of Moscow State University, but Michael was prevented from becoming an astronomer, from studying physics, and from attending graduate school because of his Judaism. He changed his area of study to mathematics.

While attending a mathematics conference in Poland, Michael realized that the family needed more intellectual and physical freedom. When Michael returned from the conference and announced his intention to emigrate, Eugenia agreed primarily for Sergey's benefit.

After the Brins applied for an exit visa, Michael and Eugenia were both fired and survived on temporary work until their visas came through. During that time, Michael taught himself computer programming while the family continued to share a 350-square-foot apartment in Moscow with Michael's mother.

In May of 1979 the Brins moved to the United States. Sergey has often expressed his appreciation to his father for bringing him to the U.S.

In 1993, Sergey graduated with honors from the University of Maryland with a Bachelor of Science degree in science and mathematics. He went on to earn a master's degree in computer science from Stanford University in Palo Alto, California.

Brin and Page met during new-student orientation at Stanford. They did not get along at all at first—in fact, each thought the other was obnoxious—but they eventually realized they had much in common and became close friends.

In the late 1990s, the two Star Trek fans were contemplating what it would take to develop an all-knowing computer like the one on the Starship Enterprise. The duo decided to take on the challenge of improving the Internet search experience. They decided that rather than sorting pages by analyzing words and their positions in the page, they would base the relevance of the page by the number of links that connected to it. Brin and Page weren't the first ones to come up with this solution, but they were the first to figure out the math and programming. Their iconic paper was titled "The Anatomy of a Large-Scale Hypertextual Web Search Engine."

They filled Page's room at Stanford with computers and tested an early prototype of Google. The pair soon moved their operation to a borrowed garage.

Brin and Page took leave from their Ph.D. studies at Stanford while they worked to expand Google. Technically, they are still on leave.

At first, Brin and Page weren't sure how to market their search engine. They resisted ads at first, but eventually decided to sell them. Today Google earns over $2 billion per year from ads.

Google took off immediately, mostly due to its user-friendly interface. Paid links are identified and there are no pop-up ads. Many users also enjoy the web site's whimsical artwork that changes on holidays and special occasions.

The company's motto of "Don't be evil" and its friendly company culture, which includes free food and encouragement to spend 20% of their time working on personal projects, encourages the brightest to apply to work for it.

Today "to Google" has become a verb used worldwide, and Google has entered the realms of maps, news, and email with its Google Maps, Google Earth, Google News, and Gmail.

When China decided to censor the information that Google could provide, the company went along with the scheme despite Brin's misgivings based on his childhood experiences with communism. Eventually, though, Google decided to take a stand and refuse to go along any further, despite the potential of losing millions of dollars of revenue and attacks on Google allegedly by Chinese officials trying to hack into its database to locate government dissidents.

After Eugenia Brin was diagnosed with Parkinson's disease, Sergey and his wife Anne's interest in genetic engineering and the human genome project expanded.

In 2004, Brin and Page launched Google.org, which aims to solve problems concerning energy and the environment. Projects include alternative and renewable energy such as an offshore wind farm, the Tesla electric car, and a car with artificial intelligence that can help drivers avoid accidents.

Brin's net worth is estimated at $17.8 billion. He and Page are tied on *Forbes*' list of the world's richest people at #24.

Sheldon Adelson

Sheldon Adelson is the chairman of casino owner and operator The Las Vegas Sands Corporation. Adelson has made and lost fortunes several times.

Adelson is married to his second wife, Dr. Miriam Adelson, a prominent authority of the treatment of drug abuse. He has five children. Adelson was born August 4, 1933, in Boston, Massachusetts, the son of a taxi driver.

When he was only 12 years old, he borrowed $200 from uncle to sell newspapers. After graduating from high school, he attended City College in New York, majoring in corporate finance and real estate, but did not graduate.

After a stint in the army, Adelson worked as a courtroom stenographer on Wall Street in the early 1960s. He earned his first million teaching companies how to sell shares on the stock market.

He moved back to Boston and began investing in companies, at one time owning up to seventy-five different firms. His most profitable business was American International Travel Service.

Adelson lost his first fortune and went deep into debt when the stock market declined in the late 1960s, but he soon rebounded by arranging condominium conversions in Boston, where he also bought a residential building. When the condo market faltered, Adelson again lost his cash.

In 1971 he acquired the majority of a small magazine publisher, among whose publications was computer magazine, *Data Communications User*. While at a condominium convention in California, he read that a magazine about condominiums had produced the show and decided to use his magazine to produce a computer show.

Adelson held his first show in 1973 in Dallas. He started The Interface Group in Needham, Massachusetts, focusing on the computer show. He soon sold his condo and share in the publishing company but kept the show. The show was growing slowly when Adelson created a new show, the Computer Dealer Expo, COMDEX, which first took place in Las Vegas in 1979. Adelson's show hit just at the right time, as personal computers were becoming a huge industry. COMDEX was intended for small computer dealers but soon grew into the largest trade show in Las Vegas with earnings of $20 million in 1984. By the late 1980s, the Interface Group was producing forty shows with a net annual income of $250 million.

In the late 1980s Adelson and his partners began looking for Las Vegas real estate. After being rejected by several owners, they bought the Sands from casino developer Kirk Kerkorian in 1988. At one time the hotel had been the most popular on the Vegas Strip, home to Frank Sinatra and his Rat Pack, but time had taken its toll. Adelson planned to renovate the Sands and build a convention center and a new resort and shopping mall, but soon gained a reputation as a stubborn, demanding boss and a union buster. He ran into opposition from the Las Vegas Convention and Visitors Authority and the Nevada State Gaming Control Board but was able to use his political connections overcome objections.

Adelson opened the Sands in 1989 but the stalled economy put expansion plans on hold. He stopped paying his creditors, including the former head of the Sands, with whom he settled out of court, and the Sands' architect, who successfully sued him for $1.3 million in 1993.

Adelson sold COMDEX to the Japanese firm Softbank for $860 million in 1995. With the profits, Adelson raised funds from Wall Street, extracted himself from Interface, and opened The Sands Expo and Convention Center. He later demolished the Sands Hotel and Casino and built the Venetian Hotel and Casino, modeled after Venice, Italy, where he and Miriam had once vacationed. Despite lawsuits by contractors and the Culinary Union, the hotel was wildly successful, and Adelson soon built the nearby Palazzo.

He successfully expanded the casino into Asian markets Macau and Singapore, although his Asian group is under investigation by the SEC for alleged bribery.

Adelson took his company public in 2004 so successfully that he leapt to number three on *Forbes*' list of the world's richest people.

Adelson plans to open more hotels under the Four Seasons, Sheraton, and St. Regis names.

Adelson's philanthropy includes the Dr. Miriam and Sheldon G. Adelson Medical Research Foundation and the Dr. Miriam and Sheldon G. Adelson Clinic for Drug Abuse Treatment and Research. He is a major contributor to Israel and the local Jewish community as well as the Republican Party.

Adelson's 2011 net worth is estimated at $23.3 billion. He is listed on *Forbes*' list at #16.

• Stefan Persson

Stefan Persson is the chairman of the board of directors and chief executive officer (CEO) of trendy retail chain H&M (Hennes & Mauritz). His father, Erling, founded the "cheap chic" H&M chain in 1947.

Persson lives in Stockholm, Sweden. He also owns the small English village of Linkenholt. He is married to Carolyn Denise Persson; they have three children. Persson was born on October 4, 1947, in Stockholm, the son of Erling and Margrit Persson.

Stefan earned an associate in arts and science degree from the University of Stockholm.

He joined H&M in 1972. Four years later he helped out at the launch of the chain's London store by standing outside and handing out ABBA records as a promotional stunt.

In 1974 the company began to be listed on the Stockholm Stock Exchange, partially to avoid paying Sweden's enormous inheritance tax. The value of H&M shares continued to increase as the company grew at a startling rate of 25% per year.

Stefan became chairman in 1979, while his father remained as CEO. Soon after taking over the reins, the younger Persson began to accelerate expansion. The company opened locations in West Germany in 1980. By 1985 there were 200 stores throughout Europe and the UK. The company began expanding into Eastern Europe in 2003.

In 1982, Stefan took over as CEO. He has a reputation for frugality. H&M employees travel coach, and the company pays cell phone bills for only a few of its executives.

Stefan presided over the company as it launched children's and maternity lines. By the end of the 1990s, H&M had become Europe's largest apparel retailer. He gave up the CEO position in 1998 but remains chairman. Stefan's son Karl-Johan, 34, took over as CEO in 2009.

H&M is known for bringing in big name designers such as Stella McCartney, Madonna, Karl Lagerfeld, and Kylie Minogue to design affordable collections for its customers and for spotting trends before they become popular. Persson also established an in-house design team at the company's Stockholm headquarters in the mid-1980s that is staffed by recent design-school graduates. At that time, manufacturing was outsourced to suppliers in countries with low labor costs such as Bangladesh, Turkey, and China.

The chain boasts 1,700 stores, including a New York store that opened in March of 2000, one in Japan that was opened in the fall of 2008, and a Los Angeles branch that opened in 2010. In 2009 the company created about 6,000 new jobs and opened 225 more stores, including its first Chinese store in Beijing.

Despite the economic recession, H&M's sales and profits continue to grow, although Persson's personal fortune has been affected adversely by the weak Euro.

Persson also serves on the boards of the Stockholm School of Entrepreneurship, Electrolux, and INGKA Holding, B.V.

He received the International Award from the United States National Retail Federation in 2000.

Stefan's charitable work includes founding the Mentor Foundation, a nonprofit organization that fights substance abuse among youth. He is famous for terminating supermodel Kate Moss' H&M's modeling contract after photos surfaced that allegedly showed the model snorting cocaine.

He is a supporter of Djurgårdens IF and is co-founder of a foundation for the club.

Persson is an avid sportsman who enjoys downhill skiing and playing golf and tennis.

His current net worth is $24.5 billion. He is Sweden's richest private citizen and, according to *Forbes*, the 13th richest person in the world.

Steve Jobs

Steve Jobs is the co-founder of Apple, Incorporated. He recently resigned as CEO but is still the chairman of the board.

Jobs was born on February 24, 1955, in San Francisco, California.

He lives with wife Laurene Powell in Palo Alto, CA. They have two children. He also has a daughter, Lisa Brennan Jobs as a result of a relationship with painter Chrisann Brennan. At first he denied paternity, swearing in court that he was sterile, but eventually admitted he was the father and paid millions in child support.

His biological parents, Joanne Simpson, an 18-year-old graduate student who later became a speech pathologist, and Abdulfattah Jandali, a Syrian graduate student who became a political science professor, put him up for adoption when he was born. The couple later got married and had a daughter, novelist Mona Simpson.

Steve was adopted as an infant by Paul and Clara Jobs of Mountain View in Northern California. The Jobs later adopted a daughter, Patti.

Paul was a Coast Guard veteran and machinist and Clara an accountant. When he was a boy, Jobs and his father worked together on electronics in the garage. He was a very intelligent child but did not do well in school.

While attending Homestead High School in Cupertino, Jobs attended lectures at Hewlett-Packard (HP) in Palo Alto where he met Steve Wozniak. Jobs once asked William Hewlett, the president of HP, for parts for a class project. Hewlett gave Jobs the parts and a summer internship.

Jobs enrolled in Reed College in Portland, Oregon, but dropped out after only one semester. He stayed, sleeping on the floors of his friends' rooms and auditing classes, including one in calligraphy, which eventually led to Jobs' insistence that his computers have multiple typefaces and proportional fonts. Jobs supported himself by recycling bottles and eating free meals at a Hare Krishna temple.

Jobs returned to California and began attending meetings of the "Homebrew Computer Club" with Wozniak and working as a technician at the Atari company. Jobs and Wozniak created and sold illegal "blue boxes" that let users make free long distance calls.

He then traveled to India with friend Daniel Kottke. Jobs returned from India broke, ill and converted to Buddhism, with a shaved head and wearing Indian clothes. He also became a pescetarian, eating fish but not meat. While in India, Jobs took LSD.

Jobs returned to Atari and worked with Wozniak on a project to create a circuit board for a video game.

The two began building computers in Jobs' garage, financing their operations by selling Jobs' Volkswagen bus and Wozniak's scientific calculator and founded Apple with funding from Intel's Mike Markkula. Jobs recruited Mike Scott from National Semiconductor to serve as CEO, a move that led to discord. Scott was soon fired from Apple.

Jobs then enticed Pepsi's John Sculley to serve as Apple CEO, asking, "Do you want to sell sugar water for the rest of your life, or do you want to come with me and change the world?"

Apple aired its iconic Super Bowl television commercial entitled *1984* in that year, and Jobs introduced the Macintosh at the annual shareholders' meeting. It was the first small computer to feature a graphical user interface. Computer sales slumped and Scully took over as head of Macintosh development.

Jobs then founded NeXT Computer. The NeXT workstation was technologically advanced but extremely expensive. It had an object-oriented software development system, a digital signal processor chip, and a built-in Ethernet port. In 1996, Apple bought NeXT for $429 million. It now focuses entirely on software.

In 1986, Jobs bought The Graphics Group, later renamed Pixar, from George Lucas for $10 million. Pixar contracted with the Walt Disney Company to make such award-winning films as *Toy Story* and *Up*. Disney bought Pixar and Jobs gained a position on Disney's board of directors and became its largest shareholder, with 7% of the stock.

The company then introduced iPod portable music players, iTunes digital music software, the iTunes Store music distribution system, the iPhone, and the iPad.

Jobs is known for wearing long-sleeved black mock turtleneck sweaters, jeans, and sneakers.

In 2004 Jobs was diagnosed with pancreatic cancer. He has taken several leaves and has received treatment, including a liver transplant. He is currently on leave to focus on his health.

There is no record of Jobs supporting any philanthropic causes. In fact, when he returned to the CEO position, he ended all existing charitable efforts. His name does not appear on any donor lists, and his charitable foundation shut down after only a year. While it is possible that he makes only anonymous donations, this would be quite rare among the world's billionaires.

After he crisscrossed the country looking for a liver for his transplant before finding one in Memphis, he persuaded California's legislators to require drivers to state on their licenses whether they want to donate their organs.

Jobs received the National Medal of Technology and was named CEO of the decade by *Fortune*.

In 2011, Jobs' wealth was estimated by *Forbes* at $8.3 billion, placing him 110th on the list of the world's richest people.

Vladimir Lisin

Vladimir Lisin is a Russian steel magnate.

Lisin was born in Ivanovo in what was then the Soviet Union on May 7, 1956.

Lisin currently lives in Moscow, Russia. He is married and has three children, Vyacheslav, Dmitry, and Alexander.

In 1979 he graduated with a bachelor's degree in engineering from the Siberian Metallurgical Institute. He went on to earn an MSc in metal engineering in 1989, an MSc in economics from the Russian Presidential Academy of National Economy and Public Administration in 1992, a doctorate in metal engineering in 1997, and a doctorate in economics from the Russian Presidential Academy of National Economy and Public Administration (RANEPA) in 2005. He wrote one PhD thesis on metallurgical engineering and another on economics.

In 1999 he became a professor at RANEPA, where he still teaches.

He started his working career in 1975 as a mechanic in a coalmine After earning his bachelor's degree, he got a job as a steelworker in the NGO Tulachermet, where he eventually became deputy chief of the shop. He has also worked as deputy chief engineer and deputy general director of the Karaganda Steel Plant, one of Kazakhstan's four largest steel plants.

After the demise of the Soviet Union, Lisin moved to Moscow, where he became a partner in the TransWorld Group (TWG) along with the powerful Cherney brothers, Mikhail and Lev, who had ties to then-President Boris Yeltsin and his political cronies. TWG was able to buy up the metal assets that the state was selling at bargain-basement prices and resell them at an enormous profit.

Lisin has often been cited as a "proletarian success story", but none other than the *Huffington Post* has alleged that members of TWG were members of or had dealings with the Russian mafia. So far Huffington's accusations have not been substantiated.

Nevertheless, Lisin became manager of the aluminum and steel factories and, when TWG broke up in 2000, Lisin acquired Novolipetsk Steel (NLMK) partially through a buyout of shares from American financier George Soros.

Towards the end of 2005, Lisin sold some of his holdings on the London Stock Exchange for $610 million, which he then used to purchase one energy company and two coal companies, intending to use them to supply raw materials for his steel mill.

His next move was to buy up several seaports and shipping and transportation companies, which he consolidated into the conglomerate Universal Cargo Logistics Holding B.V., or UCL Holding. Lisin is the sole owner of UCL.

NLMK provides raw materials to its DanSteel operation in Denmark and operates a joint venture with Duferco in Luxembourg. Additionally, it partners with companies in several countries, including France, Belgium, and the U.S.

Lisin serves as chairman of the boards of directors of OAO Novolipetsk Metallurgical Combine and the

Sayangorsky aluminum plant. He is a member of the boards of directors of the Novokuznetsk and Bratsk aluminum plant and Magnitogorsk and Novolipetsk Metallurgical Combines.

In 2007, he acquired a 14.42% stake in Bank Zenit through the offshore company Silener Management.

Lisin has also dabbled in the newspaper business and publishes the newspaper *Gazeta*, which is one of his few non-profitable ventures.

In a 2004 interview with *Forbes* magazine, Lisin attributed his personal success to working hard and being single-minded and his company's success to avoiding debt, unlike his competitors who owe billions of dollars for expensive foreign acquisitions.

He has called upon the Russian government to reduce regulations to stimulate the country's domestic growth and, ironically, he has also called for an end to government corruption.

The somewhat reclusive Lisin is known to avoid parties and politics.

Honors that Lisin has received include the Honorary Metallurgist of Russia prize, the Council of Ministers' prize in Science and Engineering, the Knight of the Order of Honour of the Russian Federation, and the Knight of the Order of St. Sergiy Radonezhsky.

A cigar aficionado and avid skeet and trap shooter, Lisin built one of the largest shooting-range complexes in Europe's Lisya Nora, near Moscow.

He also owns a collection of rare cast-iron horse sculptures made in Kasli, a town in the Urals, in the 19th century.

In 2011, Lisin vaulted to the top of the list of Russia's richest with a net worth estimated at $24 billion. *Forbes* currently lists him at #13 in the world.

• Warren Buffett

Warren Edward Buffett, CEO and primary shareholder of Berkshire Hathaway, is perhaps the most successful investor of the past century. In 2008 he was considered the wealthiest man on Earth. Since then, he has dropped to third richest man in the world, after donating several billion dollars to various charities and losing more to economic turmoil.

He is noted for his atypically modest lifestyle, given his immense wealth. He has lived in his primary residence in Omaha, Nebraska, since he purchased it in 1958 for $31,500. (Today it is valued around $700,000). He drives his own car, a Cadillac DTS. It has also been reported that Buffett does not carry a cellphone, nor does he have a computer at his desk. He and his current wife, Astrid, have stated several times that the vast majority of their estate, roughly 99% of it, will be donated to charity when they die. Buffett also is in favor of increasing taxes for the wealthiest Americans. In his own words, "Too often a vast collection of possessions ends up possessing its owner. The asset I most value, aside from health, is interesting, diverse and long-standing friends." He was married to his first wife, Susan, from 1958 until her death in 2004. He married again in 2006 to long-time friend, Astrid Menks. He and Susan had three children together.

In addition to his fervent frugality, Buffett is known for his strict adherence to an investment philosophy known as value investing. This philosophy involves investments in companies that will make the most profits in proportion to the overall value of their stock. This method can differ drastically from the more common practice of buying stocks in sheer speculation that the stocks' prices will increase.

Buffett's interest in the stock market started at an early age. By 12, he had read every stock investments book at the Omaha Public Library. He received his bachelor's degree at 19 before attending Columbia Business School in order to study under Benjamin Graham, Buffett's most highly regarded mentor to this day. There, he received a Master of Science degree in economics.

Buffett began working as a stockbroker in his home state, following advice from Graham to avoid working on Wall Street. While he was there, he also began teaching an investment principles class at University of Nebraska Omaha.

A few years later he received an invitation to work for Graham's partnership, which Buffett eagerly accepted. His work there revolved around managing investments. Graham was adamant that all purchases made by his partnership were to have a large margin of safety, a key component to value investing. Margin of safety refers to the difference between a stock's market value (how much you'd pay for a share) and its intrinsic value (a share's core value). Buffett initially questioned Graham's strict adherence to margin of safety, noting that higher profits could be made on riskier investments.

In 1956 the investment partnership closed as Graham retired. Later that year, Buffett started his own investment partnership, Buffet Partnership Ltd. By 1960 the partnership had expanded to seven separate partnerships. One of his most notable investments was Sanborn Map Company, which had a market value that was only 70% of its intrinsic value. Sanborn Maps accounted for 35% of the partnership's portfolio at the time and was a major contributor to the partnerships' early success.

In 1962, Buffett merged all seven of his partnerships into one and invested heavily in the textile firm, Berkshire

Hathaway. A few years later, the head of Berkshire Hathaway offered Buffet $11½ per share for all of Buffet's shares in order to buy the company back. However, when the official papers arrived for Buffett to sign, the price had been reduced to 11^{3}/_{8}$ without Buffet's prior approval. This angered Buffett, who in response began purchasing Berkshire shares until he himself gained control of the company. But Berkshire Hathaway was a failing company, of which Buffett was suddenly the majority shareholder. By 1985 Berkshire Hathaway no longer manufactured textiles. Its sole purpose was as a holding company.

In retrospect, Buffett claims that buying control of Berkshire Hathaway was the worst investment decision he ever made, claiming it has cost him over $200 billion in the fifty years since.

According to Forbes, Buffett's net worth was estimated to be $50 billion in March 2011.

• About Minute Help Press

Minute Help Press is building a library of books for people with only minutes to spare. Follow @minutehelp on Twitter to receive the latest information about free and paid publications from Minute Help Press, or visit minutehelpguides.com.

Printed in Great Britain
by Amazon